SCHOOL ESSAYS ON TOPICAL PROBLEMS

D1618518

120, -

DIE VERFASSERIN

Felicity ZIMMEL, geborene HOWROYD, ist seit Jahren als Lehrerin in Nachhilfe und Prüfungsvorbereitung, vor allem für Schüler der AHS, tätig. Sie lieferte auch zahlreiche Beiträge für Schulfunk-Sendungen des ORF. Im Cura Verlag hat sie neben dem vorliegenden Werk "A Student's Aid to Modern English Literature", "Everyday English Idioms" (ein lexikalisches Nachschlagewerk) und einen Band "English Exercises" (Übungen zur Festigung der englischen Grammatik) veröffentlicht, sowie an dem Buch "The Dialogue Way to Better English" (Heitere Dialoge mit Grammatikbeispielen und Übungsstoffen samt Schlüssel und Wörterverzeichnis) durch Erstellung der ÜBUNGSAUFGABEN maßgeblich mitgearbeitet.

FELICITY ZIMMEL-HOWROYD

SCHOOL ESSAYS
ON TOPICAL PROBLEMS
» S O M E I D E A S & F A C T S «

ANREGUNGEN UND DATEN FÜR
ENGLISCHE MUSTERAUFSÄTZE
ZU AKTUELLEN PROBLEMEN DER ZEIT

FÜR DIE OBERSTUFE DER AHS

CURA VERLAG WIEN

Illustrationen auf den Seiten 11, 17, 31, 52 und 57 mit freundlicher Genehmigung von PUNCH, London

6. durchgesehene und aktualisierte Auflage 1990

© 1975 by CURA VERLAG Ges.m.b.H. Wien
Alle Rechte vorbehalten
Textschrift von "brother" EM-85
Printed in Austria
Gesamtherstellung: Wiener Verlag Himberg
Das Werk trägt die ISBN 3-7027-0159-1

TABLE OF CONTENTS (INDEX)

DIESES BUCH

bietet eine Auswahl von englischen Aufsätzen über zeit-
gemäße Themen, die als M o d e l l e für die Schulung
im freien englischen Aufsatz gedacht sind. Sie sollen
eine Hilfe sein für das Abfassen von Aufsätzen und dar-
über hinaus auch Ideen und Tatsachen (Ideas & Facts)
bieten. Da sich einige Themenkreise überschneiden, er-
scheinen gewisse Passagen mehrmals in verschiedenen
Aufsätzen, um zu zeigen, daß das gleiche Vokabular für
verschiedene Themen verwendet werden kann.

In einigen Aufsätzen wurden Figuren aus der Literatur
als Beispiele für besondere Charaktereigenschaften oder
Geisteshaltungen herangezogen. Dies soll dem Lernenden
vor Augen führen, daß solche Gestalten zur Veranschauli-
chung allgemeiner Ideen benützt werden können. Jedem
Aufsatz ist eine Liste der angewendeten P h r a -
s e n angeschlossen.

Diese jedem Musteraufsatz angefügte Aufstellung wichti-
ger Wörter und Redewendungen kann für die Übung des
Studierenden unter anderem dazu dienen, mit Hilfe dieses
speziellen Wortschatzes s e l b s t ä n d i g zu dem
betreffenden Thema einen eigenen Aufsatz zu formu-
lieren.
So gebraucht, wird dieses Buch sicherlich eine wertvolle
Hilfe und Anregung für viele, die beim Abfassen eines
freien englischen Aufsatzes mit gewissen Schwierigkeiten
zu kämpfen haben.

Die Verfasserin

THE MASS MEDIA

The mass media - the radio, the cinema, TV and the press - play a very important part in modern society. Not only do they act as a bridge between the individual and the cultural and political life of his country, but they provide him with the greater part of his entertainment.

A revolutionary change in our way of life came with the development of the radio. From 1920 onward it became a fad everywhere. Amateur enthusiasts built their own sets. People without sets gathered in their friends' homes to hear this new invention. By the end of the 30's there was a wireless set in nearly every home and people began to turn to the radio for information and entertainment. Today we have portable transistors, sometimes combined with cassettes, which provide us with non-stop programmes. We can choose between broadcasts, of high cultural value (classical music, plays, lectures, etc.), regional programmes of strong local interest, and popular music, sport and hourly news broadcasts. Some youngsters cannot do without their "walkmen" which provide them wherever they go with their favourite music.

In the thirties the cinema, too, became very popular. Before World War II countless families went to their local cinema twice a week when the programme changed. People used to queue up sometimes for an hour and more to get in. In the 50s and 60s television became more popular than the cinema and many picture houses had to close down. Latterly, however, there has been an increase in the popularity of films. TV viewers, tired of the eternal series, soap operas and commercials, prefer to see good films on large screens. The remaining cinemas have been divided into three or more smaller ones, so there is always a choice of films to see. It is now possible to buy or hire cassettes of films and watch them at home on a VCR (video cassette recorder) attached to a TV set.

Some people like to see their favourite film stars, no

matter what kind of films they act in. Others read the film reviews in newspapers or magazines before they decide which film to see. But in any case Hollywood is no longer "dying" but is doing very well, some of the large studios having been bought up by Japanese investors. Cinema is big business again now because of the VCR boom.

Another popular form of entertainment today is TV.

The majority of people in industrial countries own a TV set. The chief advantage of TV is you can watch it at home. TV brings the world into your home and you need not leave your own armchair. Another advantage is that it is informative. By watching the news every day people know what is going on in the world. Politicians are interviewed and speak to the voters by means of TV; parliamentary sessions are broadcast and discussions are held about topical subjects. TV can also be instructive, with its geographical and scientific films and school TV programmes.

TV's trump card, however, is that it can show us great events while they occur; this is especially interesting in the case of international sporting events like the Olympic Games or great occasions like the landing on the moon. Many people think that TV has more disadvantages than advantages. The main effect that it produces is that owners of a set stay at home much more and tend to give up the parties, hobbies and other occupations which had previously filled their evenings. But as conversation in a darkened room is difficult, TV has a detrimental effect on family life. There is, too, a real danger that TV, by constantly showing scenes of war, crime and brutality, may make people indifferent and callous to the real problems of life, turning them into non-thinkers. Commercial TV, especially in the U.S. is used by the manufacturing sponsors to create consumer demand, and thus to "manipulate" the viewers into buying their goods.

In most Western countries, especially in Britain and the U.S., the press is in the hands of a few powerful men, who are in a position to dictate what news and views shall be published in the newspapers that are read by the majority of the population. We can distinguish between the popular press, which is sensational in style and outlay and which lays a great emphasis on scandal, crime and sport; and the serious press, which devotes much space to political news, reports on industry and financial matters. In Western-style democracies there is a high standard of journalism in the serious press. The journalist is usually a graduate with special training in the duties of a newspaper man to inform the public, to offer reasoned argument and comment without distortion of facts and to offer honest guidance. A democracy can operate successfully only on the foundation of well-informed public opinion. We, in a democracy, have the opportunity to choose among various newspapers which are "right" or "left", and we are free to make up our own minds on any question, trying to find out what is really true and whether the news has been "slanted". But people living under a totalitarian regime have no choice. The state owns all the mass media and can manipulate the population at will. The people have no other sources of information and are therefore obliged to accept the facts that are put before them.

Summing up, the mass media play an important part in our lives. It is up to us to derive not only entertainment but also information and instruction from them. We should not allow ourselves to be manipulated and we should be thankful that we have freedom of speech and of opinion.

IMPORTANT WORDS AND PHRASES

to provide (someone) with
to become a fad (craze, fashion)
to be developed
to be devoted to / to devote (much space) to
to take the trouble to
by means of (TV, the radio)
to be broadcast

honest guidance
distortion of facts
to have the opportunity to
to choose among
to make up one's mind
"slanted" (news)
at will
Summing up = To sum up = In conclusion
It is up to us

TV's trump card
..., however, ... = but...
to tend to
to have a detrimental effect on
to manipulate (someone) into (buy-)
    ing
to distinguish between
to lay emphasis on
reasoned argument

to derive (entertainment, instruc-
    tion, etc.) from (the mass-media)
to allow oneself to (be manipulated)

The sign = means an alternative word
or phrase of similar meaning; e.g.:
to support = to promote.

POLLUTION

Danger to the environment is one of the greatest problems of today. Industrialization has brought with it the
pollution of air and water and the problem of waste-
disposal. The air is polluted by the smoke from factory
chimneys and coal-driven locomotives, by the exhausts
of motor vehicles and aeroplanes, and by tiny particles
of fibres.
The amount of water on the earth - only 2 % of which
is potable - has not increased at all since the beginning
of history. Yet mankind is busy polluting it as rapidly
as possible. Chemical wastes and sewage are discharged
into the seas, rivers and lakes. Fish are killed by the
heated wastes discharged by atomic power plants. In
many places today fish contain poisonous chemicals and
are not longer fit to eat. The sea is polluted by oil,
either discharged by ships or leaking from them after
collisions. This oil is then washed on to the coast, where
it not only makes the beaches dirty and unfit for bathing
but kills all the fish, plant life and even the birds which
get caught in it. Insecticides like DDT were thought
to be a wonderful discovery, because they killed harmful
or disease-bringing insects. But recently experts have
found out that they are also dangerous because they
upset the ecology. Not only do they kill the insects,
but also the useful birds and animals that eat them;
in this way the whole balance of nature is disturbed.
These chemicals are absorbed by the soil and the crops
and later find their way into the stomachs of animals
and humans, causing cancer and other diseases.

Waste-disposal, too, has become an acute problem today. In our affluent society goods are over-packaged or sold in "one-way" containers. Articles made of plastic are not recyclable and accumulate in huge piles.

There is another aspect of environment pollution: "visual pollution". The natural beauty of our country-side is rapidly being spoilt; litter is left behind by tourists at

"We create it, we clean it up –
business couldn't be better ...!"

From PUNCH

beauty spots, and rubbish is dumped illegaly into woods and streams. Our beautiful fields, hills and mountains are criss-crossed by rows of ugly pylons carrying electric cables. The suburbs of towns and cities, with their rows of ugly little houses, are slowly eating up the country-side. Beautiful old houses or parts of villages are pulled down to make way for gigantic motorways. In the cities public parks are sacrified to make room for car parks.

Technology is responsible for all these evils, but technology can also solve our present problems. Air pollution can be checked by the installation of filters in factory chimneys and the use of smokeless fuel. Water pollution can be prevented by the installation of water-clarification plants. The problem of waste disposal can be solved by the erection of incineration plants or recycling processes.

Man's greed knows no boundaries - it results in the extinction of thousands of species of animal life, in the destruction of the rain forests, in the dangerous pollution of the air we breathe and the water we drink. The seas have become dumping grounds, the desert encroaches on farmland in Africa. We are all threatened by the imminent global warming brought about by the "greenhouse effect", and by the thinning of the ozone layer. Private organizations like Greenpeace, Global 2000 and the World Wildlife Fund do all they can to warn us.

But pollution can only be combated by strict laws and controls, rigorous enforcement, and international agreements. If the governments of the world do not act quickly mankind cannot survive.

environment
waste-disposal
exhausts of (motor vehicles)
potable = drinkable
chemical wastes
sewage
to discharge = to dump
no longer fit to (eat)
unfit for (... ing)

to upset (the ecology) = to disturb
to be absorbed
to find one's way into
affluent society
recyclable
to accumulate
litter / paper, bottles, etc.
rubbish = garbage
to be criss-crossed

to be pulled down
to be responsible for
to be checked = controlled, stopped
smokeless fuel
to be prevented
water-clarification plant

incineration plant = trash burner
re-cycling process
industrial smoke
to be combated
enforcement of (laws) / to enforce
  laws

OVERPOPULATION

Every day 350,000 babies are born. But experts are not completely pessimistic about our future - they believe that a world population of 130 billions need not necessarily starve. Whereas it took mankind millions of years to reach the billion-mark at the beginning of the 19th century, this number was doubled in the following century. Today the earth has a population of about 3.7 billions and towards the end of the century it will be about 6.5 billions.
But the UNO has now stated that the food reserves of the earth are not at all exhausted. At present our planet could feed 16 billion people from the already-cultivated areas. But as the earth's cultivated areas can be increased sixfold, a world population of 130 billions would not need to starve.
The second (1974) report of the Club of Rome - an informal group of 85 leading international businessmen, scientists and thinkers devoted to solving the problems of an ever more complicated world - is also more optimistic than pessimistic. Unlike its first report, it does not support a policy of no growth; instead, it promotes the idea of selective growth: less industrialization in the rich countries to counterbalance more in the poor nations. But it also points out the urgency of global problems. Delay will simply make matters worse. For example, the computer model shows that if birth control programmes are postponed for ten years, there will be an increase of 1.7 billion people in the developing countries alone by the year 2000. A 20-year delay would result in 3.7 billion more being born - just as many as

the earth's present population. At that point, starvation and disease would kill about the same number of people as prompt action on birth control would prevent from being born in the first place. But what a tragic difference for individual families as well as for the quality of the survivors' lives! The only way to avoid turning present "catastrophic" food shortages in India and Africa into an "apocalyptic" famine by the year 2010 is to tackle at once every aspect of the problem. First of all population must be curbed.

The main aim of all population-planners is the lowering of the birthrate. For this a knowledge of methods of birth control is essential. A lack of this knowledge can be described as "a kind of illiteracy".

How can we combat this "illiteracy"?

Experts believe that this can only be done by an intensive enlightenment campaign. Family-planning clinics should be set up in as many places as possible; not only in cities and towns, but also in the most outlying districts of both developed and developing countries - and the older children at school should be given information about birth control. In underdeveloped countries like India, it is often the fear of a destitute old age that makes people want as many children as possible. As there is no social security for the old, parents must rely on their children to support them when they can no longer work. Birth control measures should therefore go hand in hand with better social security for old people. The status of women in society must be improved. When women all over the world have a better education they can achieve a higher position in society. Then they will no longer be relegated to the kitchen and be the child-bearing machines that they still are today in many parts of the world.

The main problem that faces the over-populated world of tomorrow is famine. So scientists, instead of constructing atom bombs and interplanetary rockets, should devote their energies to discovering new sources of food.

New areas of the earth must and can be cultivated.

need not necessarily = does not
    have to
to be exhausted
to be increased (sixfold)
to be devoted to (...ing)
to support = to promote (an idea,
    a policy)
to prevent from (being)

in the first place
to tackle = to deal with (a problem)
to combat (illiteracy, overpopu-
    lation)
to go hand in hand with
to be relegated to (the kitchen,
    menial work)
to devote (one's energies) to
    (...ing)

RELATIONSHIPS BETWEEN THE GENERATIONS

In relationships between parents and children, teachers and pupils, young people and their parents' generation, the fundamental problem, in my opinion, lies in their different attitudes. Ever since the world began, the older people have been complaining about the younger generation. They have always been shocked at the behaviour of the young, at the "state of the world", at the general decline in morals. Old people always talk about "the good old days" when they were young. Looking back on their youth from a distance it seems to them to have been a happier time than the present. They forget the struggles, dreams and problems which they had then, just as other young people have now. Now that they have reached middle age, they want nothing but peace and security. To them, young people seem wild, frivolous and reckless; older people are shocked at the manners, fashions and interests of the young. When Johann Strauss played his first waltzes and the young people of Vienna went crazy about them, the older generation shook their heads and held up their hands in horror.
"What is the world coming to?" they cried, just as the parents do today who cannot understand their children's enthusiasm for beat or rock music. A hundred years ago parents were just as shocked at the young people's clo-

thes as they are today at the youngsters' ragged jeans
and long hair. The older generation is always distrustful
and suspicious of innovations.They cannot get accustomed
to achievements of technical science such as space satellites and trips to the moon. What young people take
for granted is for older people suspicious and dangerous.

In the 19th century and beginning of the 20th century,
discipline at home and at school was very strict. Children were brought up to "be seen but not heard". But
Freudian psychology revealed that many complexes and
much mental illness can be traced back to unhappiness
or bad experiences in childhood. So in the last thirty
years there has been a general movement towards "permissiveness" and anti-authoritarian upbringing. The child's
happiness is all-important, the psychologists say, but
some people think that the excessive permissiveness of
modern parents is surely doing more harm than good.
The dividing line between permissiveness and negligence
is very fine; and a child brought up in the anti-authoritarian way will surely find it difficult to adjust in later
life.
The young people of today are more spoilt than their
elders were. They have more money and leisure than
ever before. Some are therefore tempted to waste their
time; they hang about the streets, turn to vandalism
out of boredom, and sometimes drift into a life of crime. The youth of today is disillusioned. After two world
wars and the breakdown of empires they have few ideals
left. They feel betrayed by politicians, and they despise
the materialistic "rat-race" of their parents. So a minority reacts by demonstrating against the "Establishment"
and by supporting anarchy. Many practise forms of "es-
capism". They try to escape from reality by taking drugs
like LSD, marihuana, or even cocaine or heroin.
They "drop out" of modern life with its materialistic
ideals. They live in the present as they have grown
up under the shadow of the atom bomb, under the constant threat of complete annihilation. In spite of this

disillusionment, however, there are many other young
people who have found more positive ways of expressing
their dissatisfaction at today's world and who seek to
change it by other methods. They join voluntary organizations and work for practical solutions of social and
economic injustice. Some run youth clubs in the slum
districts, for instance, and others go to work in the
developing countries.

The older generation will always be more conservative
than the younger generation. As older people have more
experience of life, they are distrustful and afraid of
change. For them, security lies in tradition. Young people, on the other hand, are bold and daring. They do

*"Maurice has a wonderful understanding with the child-
ren - they don't understand him and he doesn't try
to understand them..."*

From PUNCH

not think of risks and dangers and are ready to try anything new. So there will always be a difference in attitude between the generations. But this does not mean
that there cannot be more understanding.

the (basic, fundamental) problem lies in	negligence
to be shocked at	to be spoilt
to go crazy about	to be tempted to
to get accustomed to	to turn to (vandalism, crime, drugs)
to take for granted	to drift into
to be brought up	disillusioned, disillusionment
to reveal = to show up	rat-race
to be traced back to	to react by (...ing)
permissive, permissiveness	to drop out
anti-authoritarian	in spite of
to do more harm than good	to find ways of (...ing)
	to join (an organization, a club)
	to run (a club, a shop, a business)

HOW CAN WE HELP THE DEVELOPING COUNTRIES ?

In his encyclica Against Poverty (Populorum Progressio)
Pope Paul VI said that is was the duty of the industrial
or "developed" nations to help the poorer or "developing"
ones. The USA and Canada, for example, have done much
to help the starving people of India and Africa by sending them huge quantities of grain. International organizations, such as the Red Cross, U.N., and UNICEF, or
charitable institutions, such as Caritas, collect money
and send food, clothes and medicaments to famine-stric-
ken districts. Sending only such aid is not enough, however. Firstly, it does not always reach the people for
whom it is destined, but gets diverted on the way and
is sold on the black market. Secondly, it trains the recipients of aid to be dependent. They change their old
traditional way of life - they were nomads, farmers,
etc. - and now live idly in camps waiting to be fed.
Developing countries need schools and teachers. We can
help them by building schools and training centres and
by sending them teachers and teaching material.

Austria, for example, has built schools in South America which are attended by the local population and where Austrian teachers work. Later, native teachers can continue the work. Or we can provide the means for students from developing countries to study in Austria. After they have finished their training here they go back to their home countries and work as craftsmen, nurses, doctors, engineers and so on, or teach their fellow-countrymen themselves. Education alone can raise their standard of living and help them to be independent.

We can also send engineers and craftsmen to help them to build power stations, factories and other means of production. But it is most important for them to have their own trained experts who can carry on the work after the foreigners have left. Agricultural experts can also do much to help the developing countries. They can teach the natives modern methods of agriculture. For instance, the villagers in South Africa formerly used to plough up and down hill, but when the rains came, good fertile soil was washed away. Foreign experts taught them to plough around the hills so that the soil was saved. These experts also do research and can teach them which kind of rice, tobacco or sugar-cane grows best in tropical countries.

Because of over-population the people of the developing countries are faced with famine. They must therefore be informed of the dangers of the population explosion. Family-planning clinics should be set up in all districts and people should be given information about modern methods of birth control. Through better education facilities the status of women should be improved; social reforms should provide people with security in their old age.

We must help the developing countries, not only because they are poor but in order to preserve world stability and peace. Poor and starving peoples are always a threat to stability because they are breeding-grounds of revolution. We need a stable world economy and we need the developing countries as markets for our own goods.

To sum up, population must be curbed, and there must be quicker planting, economic investment and worldwide development of industry.

The result would be a truly interwoven global economic system in which all nations helped one another for mutual gain.

to help by (send)ing
to be destined for (the starving people)
to get diverted
the recipients of aid
to provide the means for
because of = on account of = owing to
to be faced with

to be informed of
to provide (people) with
a threat (danger) to
breeding-grounds of revolution
To sum up = Summing up = In conclusion
to be curbed
for mutual gain = benefit

MY RESPONSIBILITIES TOWARDS OTHERS

"Am I my brother's keeper...?"

According to Christian morals every man is his brother's keeper and we are all to some extent responsible for the happiness of our fellow men. Unselfishness, consideration and helpfulness towards others are among the finest qualities of human character. A person who has not been brought up to be considerate to others is selfish, ruthless and disliked by most of his fellow men. The hated and cruel tyrants of history have been overthrown, and aggressive nations have eventually been defeated for the same reason.

When the Industrial Revolution brought the rapid development of industry in the 19th century, it also brought with it many new problems. Above all, an enormous new class was created - the working class. And these people were usually badly paid and badly housed. When bad times came, they lost the small wage that was their only possession and they became absolutely destitute.

In former times, when society was mainly agricultural,

problems such as unemployment, old age or the care of the sick did not arise. Families lived in the country; there was plenty of work for everyone, and if a member of the family was old, sick or helpless he was cared for by the others. But the Industrial Revolution changed all this: people who are themselves badly housed and badly paid cannot care for their poorer and older relatives. Something had to be done to help these people. The work of private charities was not enough; it became clear that the state must take on the responsibility for the care of the old, the sick, the unemployed and the destitute. Trade unions fought to get better conditions for the working men and the citizens of today's welfare states enjoy security from "the cradle to the grave". The state provides free education, children's benefits, mothers' benefits, health insurance, unemployment benefits and old-age pensions. In many industralized countries the local authorities - city councils - have taken over the responsibility of building homes for the working population in an effort to abolish the "slums", badly built, unhealthy dwellings erected by unscrupulous speculators during the Industrial Revolution.

In spite of all these reforms carried out by Welfare States, there is still room for private charity and voluntary organizations. Much individual effort is still needed to combat poverty and distress in our own country. It is the duty of each one of us to help those fellow-beings who are not as fortunate as ourselves, for instance, the blind, the deaf and dumb, orphans, refugees, or victims of natural disasters such as fire and floods.

In big cities today many people suffer from loneliness. They live in isolation and do not know their neighbours. We should not forget these lonely people and we should try to help them.

In his play "An Inspector Calls" Priestley shows how all the members of a rich family, by their selfishness and indifference, are responsible for the suicide of a poor girl. The Inspector, who is the voice of conscience, points out that it is not right just to "mind one's own business" but that we are all "members of one body".

It is also the duty of the richer nations of the world to help the poorer countries. Aid to developing countries is one of the most important issues in the world today. Not only do governments help by sending food and technical experts, but individuals can also help by collecting money at home for some special project, e.g., the sending of much needed trucks to a famine zone, or special equipment to a hospital. Young people can volunteer to work in the developing countries for one or two years.

In my opinion it is true that every man is his brother's keeper and we are all to some extent responsible for the happiness of others. So it is our duty to do as much as possible to help the less fortunate.

```
to be responsible for          to be cared for
to some extent                 to be needed
to be brought up               to combat (poverty, misery, hunger)
to be badly paid               selfishness
to be badly housed             indifference
to become destitute            to help by (send)ing
                               to volunteer to (work)
```

THE WELFARE STATE

As a result of the Industrial Revolution great industrial cities sprang up in the last century and the workers who flocked in from the country formed a new class - a huge working proletariat. In former times, when society was mainly agricultural, problems such as unemployment, or old age did not arise. Families lived on the land; there was plenty of work for everyone, and if a member of the family was old or sick he was cared for by the others.
But the Industrial Revolution changed all this: people who are themselves badly housed and badly paid cannot

care for their poorer or older relatives. Women and even children, whose wages were lower than those of the men, were forced to work in mines and in factories. When bad times came the workers lost the small wage which was their only possession, and became destitute. Something had to be done to help these people.

So in the 19th century trade unions were founded to protect workers against exploitation by their employers, to organize the fight for higher wages and to guarantee decent working conditions. The unions have played a large part in the creation of the modern Welfare State.

In the course of a long struggle the following reforms have been achieved: the prohibition of child labour and hard labour for women, a basic minimum wage, shorter working hours, free education, paid holidays, the right to a certain sum of money in the case of dismissal, health insurance, mothers' benefits, children's benefits, unemployment benefits, and old age insurance.

Today workers in Great Britain and most Western countries enjoy benefits and services which are paid out of general taxation and contributions made by employers and employees. An employee and his entire family are provided for in the event of sickness, accidents, unemployment or death. In all family matters "from the cradle to the grave" he can claim financial help from the State and when he retires from work he will receive a pension.

If we compare the situation of a worker in a Welfare State today with the conditions prevailing before World War II, or in most of the developing countries at the present time, we can see that his standard of living is much higher and that he is not a victim of insecurity. In the years between the two world wars the workers in Europe and America experienced the terrible hopelessness of the thirties, the constant fear of unemployment, and the misery of life on the "dole", the unemployment relief that was barely enough to support life.

But the social reforms of the Welfare State, whose aims

are a just distribution of income, social security and equality of opportunity, have not solved all our problems of today. For example, the trade unions often resort to strikes to enforce their claims and thus many millions of working hours are lost every year in Great Britain and the USA alone. Social reform in Great Britain with its watchword "Equality of opportunity" has not led to a classless society; on the contrary, many people think that class-consciousness is stronger in Britain today than in any other country, with many of the British still regarding society as being divided into five distinct classes. Industrialized states suffer from the worldwide problem of pollution; and the Welfare State has not solved the problem of race-discrimination nor of unemployment. Nevertheless, the main beneficiaries of the social revolution and the Welfare State are the workers. Rising wages have improved their living standard, and they enjoy a degree of social security which they never had before.

to spring up
to flock in = to pour in
to be cared for
to be badly paid
to be badly housed
to become destitute
to be founded
to play a large part in
to be achieved
to be provided for

conditions prevailing / conditions which prevailed
to be a victim of
to experience = to suffer
to support life
to resort to (strikes, violence)
on the contrary
neverthless
to enjoy (a degree of social security, a higher standard of living)

RACIAL PROBLEMS - NOT ONLY IN AMERICA

When we think of the race problem we usually connect it in our minds with the U.S. The problem originated there when blacks were brought to the American continent to work on the cotton, sugar and tobacco plantations. These wretched creatures were captured in their native Africa, brought to the coast and shipped in chains to America. Here they were bought and sold like animals and often treated with great brutality by their masters. They could stand the hot climate of the Southern States better than white people, but they were not paid for their work on the plantations.

Gradually a widespread feeling developed that slavery was wrong. The book "Uncle Tom's Cabin" (1851) aroused sympathy for the slaves all over the world. But as the Southerners were especially interested in keeping slaves to work on their large plantations, a conflict arose with the anti-slavery North, finally leading to the American Civil War and the abolition of slavery in 1865.

The blacks were at last free, but they still did not have the same rights as white men. Segregation was still practised in the South; the blacks had to attend their own schools and churches, and were not allowed into the white men's hotels and restaurants. It was only after the passing of the Civil Rights Act under President Johnson (1964) that segregation was made illegal. But in the U.S. many white people still pratise a "passive" segregation and the blacks still feel discriminated against. They mostly live in ghettos, in slums in the centres of the cities which are breeding-grounds of violence and crime. They feel under-privileged because they do not have the same chances of getting as good jobs as the whites. They have become embittered because of their long hopeless struggle and because of the assassination of their leader, Martin Luther King. Militant groups like the Black Panthers preach violence against the hated whites; and some extremists of the Black Power movement demand to have a state of their own within the United States.

The race problem, however, is not only confined to America. In South Africa there is also a race problem, but its origins are different. The first white settlers came two or three hundred years ago and gradually built up a flourishing industry with gold and diamond mines. They built beautiful cities and cultivated great farms and estates. But they exploited the natives by using them only for menial work. The whites destroyed the old tribal system but did not give the natives anything to replace it. The villagers are attracted to the big cities but there are not enough jobs for them and many drift into a life of crime, unemployment and prostitution. There are not enough houses for them and so many live in miserable shanty towns.

The government of South Africa has tried to solve the problem, not by integration and equal chances for all, but by "apartheid" or segregation. This means that blacks are treated as inferiors by the whites. So they must live in special districts, must attend special schools and churches, are not even allowed to sit on the same park benches or to use the same seats in buses or trains as the whites. They are not allowed to go into the same hotels, cinemas or restaurants, or to take part in the same sporting events. For this reason South Africa had to leave the British Commonwealth of Nations and there is widespread hostility towards the government because of its racial policy.

The whites in South Africa think they are justified in not allowing the blacks to vote because if they had the right to elect their own representatives, they would be in the majority and would soon force the whites to leave the country. In other African states, where the natives have gained their independence, there has been much corruption, violence, bloodshed and civil war. So the whites of South Africa think they are right to keep the power in their own hands. But changes are slowly coming and there is hope that the blacks will finally win the right to vote.

In many other countries, however, it is the minority which is discriminated against. Then the race problem is based on prejudice and false nationalism. If there are differences of class, mentality, religion or language as, for instance, between the foreign workers in Austria and the local inhabitants, a solution can only be found by providing equal housing and education facilities, by improving living standards, and by trying to understand one another's problems. Hate and violence do not lead to a solution, but only to destruction and more violence. The idea that one race is superior to another is basically wrong, and the problem will not be solved until people recognize that all men are really equal.

to connect (something) in one's mind with
to originate
to arouse sympathy
to practise segregation / apartheid
to be made illegal
to discriminate against / to be discriminated against
breeding-grounds
underprivileged
to have the same chances of (...ing)

to become embittered
to preach violence
to be confined to
integration
to be treated as inferior(s)
widespread hostility towards
to be justified in (...ing)
to be in the majority
to gain one's independence
the struggle for survival
to be based on
to find a solution by (...ing)

THE BLACKS IN AMERICA

The abolition of legal slavery at the end of the American Civil War (1865) meant that blacks could no longer be bought and sold, that they could change their jobs and were legally in a position to claim adequate wages. But at first they were not well equipped for freedom in an equal society. Few of them had been able to learn to read and write; as slaves they had not been able to share in the American ideal of the self-made man, getting the reward of his own work in a society of equal opportunity. Also, the whites in the Southern states did not welcome them into their society. They did not regard the blacks as equals and this attitude has survived into our own time, particularly in the countryside and in small towns.

Federal action has gradually compelled the white majority in the south to allow blacks to enjoy human and civic rights, as far as these can be guaranteed by laws, but the legal protection has not solved the social problems. Social and economic discrimination survives in many forms.

The first device of equal citizenship is the right to vote. But during the period of reconstruction after the Civil War, some states passed laws that no person was to be allowed to vote if his grandfather had been a slave. Since the great majority of blacks were illiterate, tests of literacy excluded them from voting. Also, most southern states made use of the poll tax, by which people had to pay a small fee to be registered - and nearly all blacks were too poor to pay this. Now the Supreme Court has ruled that such tests and taxes are against the Constitution.

But even when legal restrictions were removed blacks still had to face hostility or intimidation, so that most of them did not dare to register or to vote. Federal agents have been used in the south to see that people are allowed to use their rights, and many cases of intimidation or abuse of power have been punished. It is only in the last few years that large numbers of southern blacks really have begun to vote and to have an influence on state and local elections and policies. Blacks in general still suffer from educational disadvantages, particularly in the south. There, separate public schools were provided for white and coloured children and each state has at least one black university. But in 1954 the Supreme Court decided that the whole system of separate education in the south was denying the constitutional right of equal treatment to the blacks, and the educational authorities were ordered to integrate their schools. The process has been slow and difficult, accompanied sometimes by riots and violence; and the social separation between the races in the south has remained very great.

In the northern states the schools have been integrated for a long time but there is still no general mixing of races. Blacks are concentrated in the central areas of big cities, so the schools in such districts have almost entirely black pupils. On the other hand, many schools in the suburbs have no black pupils. Efforts have been made to achieve integration by forced "busing" of children from one district to another but this has led to violent opposition from both blacks and whites.

Blacks who have moved to the north are in some ways worse off than those who have stayed in the south.
Some live in wretched conditions and they are outsiders in communities where they have no accepted role. The black districts are full of crime and violence. Police violence only causes more violence in its turn. Extreme right-wing political movements in the north are in favour of harsh measures against radicalism of all kinds, including all black protest. Among the blacks themselves similar extremist movements have developed. They reject all forms of progress towards equality with whites; they are in favour of "black power", taking a position that "black is right and white is wrong". In one form this movement preaches a kind of Apartheid: black areas, but controlled by black authorities; black schools, under separate control, with the children learning African history and black culture, even African language, industry and commerce run mainly by black people for black customers. Other black extremists openly advocate violence, shooting, burning and destruction, attacking all existing authority. Today, when much progress is being made towards the improvement of their conditions, this progress is damaged by some movements of black extremism, and by a renewed hostility from large parts of the white population, in reaction to campaigns for black rights or demands.
By now, especially in the south, the main problem are not so much concerned with their legal rights, but with the treatment of blacks as human beings in economic and social matters.

to be in a position to
to be equipped for
to share in
to regard ... as equals
to compel = to force

to enjoy (rights)
the right to (vote)
Since = As = Because
to be excluded from (...ing)
to make use of

to face (hostility, intimidation)
to suffer from (disadvantages)
to be provided for
at least
to deny (the right of equal treat-
    ment) to
to integrate / to be integrated
almost entirely
"bussing"

to lead to (opposition)
to be worse off than
to be in favour of
harsh measures
apartheid
to advocate (violence)
to be damaged by
in reaction to
By now = At the moment = At present
to be concerned with

S P O R T   A N D   I T S   I M P O R T A N C E

Sport has always played an important part in the life
of man. In the legends of Ancient Greece many of the
heroes were great athletes like Hercules and Achilles.
The Olympic Games were considered so important by
the Greeks that they reckoned time by that event. The
Games took place every four years and were a partly-
religious, partly-sporting festival with running races, cha-
riot races, discus-throwing and wrestling. The champion
athletes were much admired by the population and held
honoured positions in society. The Romans also attached
much importance to sport, but during the time of the
Roman Empire sporting events often degenerated into
cruel spectacles in which gladiators had to fight to the
death.
The word "sport", which first appeared in England in
the 15th century, is derived from the Latin verb "dis-
portare", meaning to amuse oneself. So the word inclu-
ded originally all sorts of amusements such as dancing,
acting, fishing, card playing etc. Sport was formerly
a pastime which only the aristocracy, the rich, could
practise. The peasants had no right to go in for sport
nor time to do so, they had to do the work which was
despised by their masters. With the gradual development
of towns, a new rich middle class grew up. They also
used their leisure and money to go in for sport. The
famous English public schools were mostly founded during the 19th century in order to train the sons of the

rising middle class in the art of leadership. At that time the British Empire was at its peak and good leaders, officers and administrators were needed to send to the colonies. The aim of the public schools has always been to produce the "ideal Christian gentleman". Much importance is attached in English schools to sport and especially to team games. Playing in a team, the boys learn to play not for personal glory, but for the good of the team as a whole. They learn loyalty, endurance and the community spirit.

There are many phrases in English connected with sport that are used in everyday life. A "team", for instance, means a group of people, such as scientists, working towards a common end or "goal". "To play the game" means to act fairly; "that is not cricket" means that it is unfair or dishonest. "To be a good loser" means that one does not show anger or disappointment if one is not successful in some enterprise.

"To pull one's weight" was originally connected with

"I've warned you before about your language!"

From PUNCH

rowing, but now means to do the necessary work and not to leave it to others.

There are also many historical anecdotes connected with sport in the English language. When Sir Francis Drake, for instance, was informed that the Armada had been sighted in the Channel, he was just having a game of bowls. He said: "There's time to finish the game and beat the Spaniards yet." The Duke of Wellington said that "the battle of Waterloo was won on the playing-fields of Eton." By this he meant that his officers had the necessary qualities for leadership because they had had a hard training at the famous public school.

Sport in ancient times was also an essential part of education, but only for a small upper class of the population. Gymnastics were part of training for war, just as team games have been used as part of training for leadership. Up to the 19th century only the ruling classes could afford to go in for sport but then the industrial revolution and social reforms brought with them a higher standard of living for the masses, better education and shorter working hours. Nowadays sport is not the privilege of a few but has become popular among the masses. Now people in all walks of life can afford to go swimming, skiing, rowing etc.

In our days the life of an average town-dweller is very unhealthy. He drives to and from his work, and spends his day sitting at an office desk or standing behind a counter or at a machine. So it is most important for health to go in for some active sport during leisure hours in order to counteract this sedentary way of life.

Not all types of sport, however, are healthy; some, like boxing or motor-racing, can be unhealthy and even dangerous. Some spectators of sport become ruthless fanatics and abuse the losers or attack the referees. This trait is condemnable and such people are like the cruel spectators at the Roman arenas, crying out for the victims' blood.

Finally it should be mentioned that the modern Olympic Games, revived in 1896 by a Frenchman, Pierre de Coubertin, are the most important sporting events in the world. People of all countries take part in them and compete fairly for the honour of winning gold, silver and bronze medals. The Games contribute very much towards international understanding. The participants are amateurs who, to reach the high level of ability required, have had to go through a very hard training and to give up a lot of things. They go to the Games full of high expectations and if these are not realized they must hide their disappointment and be good losers.

Summing up, we can say that sport plays a very important part in our lives - it is essential for our health, good for character training and a means to further international understanding. As the Romans said, the ideal for man to achieve is "mens sana in corpore sano", a healthy mind in a healthy body.

to play a part in
to be considered (important)
to attach much importance to / importance is attached to
to degenerate into
to be derived from
to practise (a pastime, a hobby)
to go in for (sport)
the art of leadership
at its peak
to be needed
to be connected with

to be an essential part of
to bring with (it, them)
to become popular among
all walks of life
to counteract
sedentary way of life
to contribute towards
Summing up = To sum up = In conclusion
a means to (further, promote) / a means of (furthering)
to achieve (an ideal, an aim)

AMERICANS AND THE AMERICAN WAY OF LIFE

America is a very young country but she cherishes her traditions, her history, and the men who made her what she is. To understand the Americans we must know a little of American history. The first settlers were mostly adventurers, or religious or political refugees from Europe; they were all courageous people, willing to brave the dangers of the New World in order to live free and better lives. This spirit of independence later led the colonists to break with Great Britain and form the United States of America. They were not willing to be dictated to by a distant parliament, and their slogan was "No taxation without representation".
In protest against the British taxes some colonists threw a cargo of tea into Boston harbour and when the British sent troops to keep order, the War of Independence broke out and a new nation was born.
About two hundred years ago the first trail blazers crossed the Appalachian mountains and the covered wagons of the pioneers braved the loneliness of the prairie and the Indians. It is only about hundred years ago since the American West was conquered by the white man. The pioneer spirit is therefore much admired by the Americans and the time of the "Wild West" is glorified in films and books. Women are not treated as inferiors but have an exalted place in society because women were in the minority in the old pioneering days. That is why it is not beneath an American man's dignity to help in the house or push the baby carriage. According to American TV programmes shown in Europe, everything centres around "Mom". American fathers seem only to bring in the dollars, mind the children and do the dishes.

The trails through the vast "Wild West" had hardly been blazed when a new type of pioneer began to open up the hidden treasures of America's raw materials. New opportunities of power were opened to a new type of

man - the self-made man. (Carnegie, Rockefeller, etc.)
The Americans now had a new ideal - the poor boy who
became a millionaire in the land of the unlimited opportunities.
When they hear the word "America", most people think
of sky-scrapers and New York, of Chicago, San Francisco,
of the film metropolis Hollywood and Henry Ford's enormous car factories. But in driving across the American
continent the foreign visitor realizes that the U.S. is
the country of thousands of small towns, with small houses lining the "Main Street". In these towns there are
three or four drugstores, one or two movie-theatres,
a super-market and a department store. American houses
are one or two stories high, usually made of wood and
have no walls or hedges. The front lawns stretch along
the whole street and in summer the front porch becomes
the main family sitting-room.
There is a great deal of running to and fro between
neighbours - a relic of the old days when the pioneer-
families helped one another and the small town was a
real community. "Babbit", although written about fifty
years ago by the American writer Sinclair Lewis, still
represents the attitude of many middle-aged Americans,
especially in the smaller towns of the Mid-West. Such
a man is still confident of his position as a good father
to his family and a public-spirited citizen. He worships
personal success, judges a man by the size of his income and believes in progress. He is not intellectual
or artistic; nor does he have much culture or taste of
his own. He supports the idea of the family, the basic
foundation of his civilization, and he is very patriotic,
believing the U.S. to be the greatest and most important
country in the world. Such a man is a member of America's "silent majority".
But America's image today has been badly damaged by
the war in Vietnam, Watergate and other scandals. (In
his book "The Quiet American" the English writer Graham
Greene described the kind of American who led his country into that war. Pyle is a "typical" American with

his Puritan conception of morality but he does not understand the Asian mentality at all. His intentions are high-minded and honourable but he has got all his ideas from books. He wants to raise a Third Force in Vietnam to destroy Communism, but he does not realize that the leader and his followers are corrupt. He refuses to listen to the advice and warnings of the more experienced English reporter, Fowler, who has lived in the country for about twenty years. Pyle's underground aid scheme only leads to more violence and finally to his own horrible murder.)

Large sections of the American population of today are no longer sure of the ideal - of the "American way of life". They feel that there is no real equality in America, although the Constitution declares that "all men are born equal". The blacks, the Indians and other minority groups feel that they are discriminated against. They do not have the same chances in life as the whites and so they are angry and embittered.
There have been the terrible assassinations of President John Fitzgerald Kennedy, Martin Luther King, and Robert Kennedy; there have also been black riots and student protest demonstrations. A small part of the young generation is so disappointed that life is not all enjoyment that they try to escape into a world of drugs. But Americans at least live in a democracy and are free to criticize what is wrong in their country. On the whole they still have the pioneering spirit. They do not only build rockets and computers, they want to build a better America, too.

to cherish (traditions)
to brave (the dangers, the loneliness)
spirit of independence
to be dictated to
to protest against
trail blazers
covered wagons
pioneers
poineer spirit
to be admired
to be glorified
to be treated as inferiors

to centre around
self-made man
land of unlimited opportunities
a great deal of (much) running to and fro
to be confident of
public-spirited
to judge (...) by
to believe in
silent majority
high-minded
to lead to (violence)
to be discriminated against

an exalted place in society
to be beneath one's dignity to
according to

to have the same chances as
to escape into
at least
to be free to

THE ENGLISH

The fact that Britain is an island has been an important factor in forming the character and shaping the destinies of the nation. The sea has protected the English, not only from military invasions, but also from the full impact of revolutionary upheavals.
But since the end of the Second World War a "silent revolution" has been carried out by reforms, the main aims of which are a just distribution of income, social security and equality of opportunity.
This democratisation, however, has been retarded by the class-consciousness of the British population. This still determines very largely the Englishman's behaviour and his attitude toward his fellow-countrymen. Many British people still regard society as being divided into five distinct classes: upper (nobility and landed gentry), upper-middle (the great industrial and merchant families, the Public School educated men), lower-middle (shop assistants, clerks, commercial travellers, lower civil servants), upper-working (skilled workers, craftsmen) and lower-working (semi-skilled and unskilled workers, heavy labourers).
The decline of the upper class and the upper-middle class began after the First World War. Britain owed vast sums to the United States, she had lost many of her oversea markets, and the financial burden of reconstruction fell on these two classes. Heavy taxes and death duties were imposed and many of the rich had to give up their "stately homes" or open them to the public. That these two classes have not vanished altogether is due to the fact that class in Britain is not simply determined by birth, wealth, and occupation, but also by education.

Upper and upper-middle class parents, wishing to preserve their position in English society, send their sons to Public Schools even though such an education is very expensive. These famous old schools are in reality private boarding schools. They aim to educate a boy to be a "Christian gentleman", train him to be a leader, give him something more than mere book-learning, namely character training. Boys are taught on the sports ground how to play fairly, how to bear pain with a "stiff upper lip", how to act as a loyal member of a team. They learn to obey as fags (personal servants) of the older boys, and later, when they are prefects, they are given authority over the younger boys, are taught to take responsibility and to exercise self-discipline. Even though the Public schools are often criticized for isolating their boys in snobbish communities, they enjoy an immense prestige in England and Public School educated men have a political influence out of all proportion to their number.

For centuries Britain was an agricultural land in which the nobility and the landed gentry (or property owners) lived in luxurious mansions in the country. During the Industrial Revolution and rise of the British Empire, Britain became the leading power and the richest country in the world. Within a few generations the new upper-middle class, comprised of the great industrial und merchant families, succeeded in becoming indistinguishable from the descendants of the feudal aristocracy. These self-made men did not settle in the ugly industrial towns which had made them rich but chose to live in large suburban houses or in the country. — Although Britain is one of the most urbanized states in the world, it is still the typical Englishman's dream to "retire to a little place in the country". If he cannot do this, he at least has a small garden around his house which he takes great pride in cultivating.

"My home is my castle" is a favourite English saying and this means that an Englishman likes his home life to be private. He erects a high wall or fence around his garden. He "keeps himself to himself" and "minds his own business". His love of privacy is reflected in his dislike of personal questions or of conversations with strangers on trains. When travelling he likes to hide behind his newspaper.

A foreign observer in Britain would find the main characteristics of the English common people to be conservatism, respect for the law, gentleness (the lack of pushing and quarrelling, the willingness to form queues), suspicion of foreigners, sentimentality about animals, exaggerated class distinctions and an obsession with all sports. The traditional Englishman is phlegmatic and unimaginative, he dislikes hysteria and fuss, admires stubbornness, and willingly accepts the bulldog (an ugly, stupid, stubborn beast) as his national emblem!

Today, four main tendencies are transforming British attitudes and institutions.

First, personal power at all levels has tended to be replaced by the impersonal power of administrative bodies.

Secondly, English society has become urbanized.

Thirdly, the technological revolution is bringing automation and rationalisation to many departments of industry. (Prosperity and full employment in Britain now depend completely on industry.)

Fourthly, democratic principles are being increasingly applied to almost every sector of British life. As mentioned at the beginning, "equality of opportunity" has been the watchword of social reform. All the amenities of civilized life (education, housing, etc.) are available to everybody.

In spite of the class-consciousness of the British population, in recent times there has been a trend towards classlessness. In the "new" (satellite) towns the sense of class hardly exists, while comprehensive schools and the new universities (built in the second half of the 20th century) are specifically intended to promote the breakdown of the old distinctions. The "technological revolution", which demands a new sort of labour force, is also playing its part in modernizing British society. Receiving

a free Grammar School education and university scholar-
ships, more and more men have risen from the lower
classes to get leading positions in politics and industry.
Since industrial competition in the international field
is keener than ever, Britain needs her best brains, no
matter from which social class they may come.
In conclusion, I must not forget to add that the English
cherish individuality, even eccentricity, and that most
of them have a good sense of humour. They possess a
nonsense literature of their own (Lewis Carroll, Edward
Lear) and often make fun of their own national characteristics, attitudes and institutions.

to be an important factor in
  (...ing)
the full impact = effect = influence
revolutionary upheavals = sudden
  changes
just distribution of income
social security
equality of opportunity
..., however, ... = but ...
to be retarded by
class-consciousness
to regard = to consider (society)
  as (...ing)
to impose (taxes, duties)
to be due to the fact that
to be determined by
even though = although

to be given authority over
to take responsibility
to exercise self-discipline
to enjoy prestige
to succeed in (...ing)
indistinguishable from
to be applied to
watchword = slogan
a trend towards
to be intended to
to play one's part in (...ing)
no matter
to cherish = to like
a sense of humour
to make fun of

Development of Society?

K. Arnold (1922) in
*   "Simplizissimus"*

DEMOCRACY

Democracy is the form of government which is best defined in Abraham Lincoln's words: "A government of the people, by the people, for the people."

Democracy, originally a Greek word, means "rule by the people" and was used by the ancient Greeks to denote a small state ruled according to the will of the people gathered together in one assembly. It was very different from the other forms of government: oligarchy, which was "rule by a few men"; aristocracy, "rule by one or more of the noble families"; plutocracy, "rule by the rich", or tyranny, "rule by one man".

The greatest enemy of democracy today is the totalitarian state in which the government is not controlled by the people, but the people are controlled by a pyramid of rulers who have seized power with the help of their armed political party. At the top of the pyramid of rulers is a single man - the Leader or Dictator - who takes upon himself all the powers of parliament and more, and who demands the total strength and blind obedience of the people in the name of the State.

Political differences cannot be tolerated; any persons who might oppose him, such as men of democratic ideas, are exiled, imprisoned, starved, worked to death, or simply killed. Open criticism is intolerable to the dictator or to the totalitarian regime and therefore dangerous to the life and liberty of the critic.

In his political satire "Animal Farm", George Orwell shows how a group of pigs seizes power after a revolution, their leader being Napoleon. Gradually he eliminates all opposition and life under his regime becomes just as cruel and hard as it was before the revolution. All opposition is crushed, and the dogs, trained as the secret police, intimidate the other animals who now live in a typical dictatorship.

On the other hand, criticism and discussion are essential features of a true democracy. A modern democratic government is representative. Nations have become too large for the people to take part themselves in the government. They therefore elect their representatives at regular intervals and the party with the majority of votes forms the government. But this does not mean that the strongest party can do what it likes. It is subjected to constant criticism, and all parliamentary measures and proposed laws must be discussed and voted on by the other representatives before they become law.

The people have a right to know what their representatives are doing. Democracy requires a well-educated and well-informed people, so a high standard of education and objectivity of the mass media are important. A democratic community must control its political passions and be able to meet political opponents in a civilized way; the right of every person to his own opinion must be respected. Democrats must be able to speak to each other and exchange ideas but this freedom must not be abused. Today small groups of political terrorists aim at abolishing it.

Democracy without personal liberties is impossible. Freedom of religion and conscience, freedom of speech and of the Press, freedom to live where one wants, the right to property - all these are basic rights of democracy. Freedom of speech and of the Press mean the right to discussion. All the arguments for and against a certain policy or event can be freely discussed in a democracy, so that the individual can form his own opinion and act accordingly. So democracy is a responsibility and a task, which is given to each individual in small as well as large things, every day anew. If a nation is equal to this task, then democracy means a dignified and decent communal life in freedom, peace, order and justice.

to be defined
according to
to be controlled by
to take upon oneself
blind obedience
to be dangerous to (life, liberty)

to eliminate (opposition)
to crush (opposition)
to intimidate
to take part oneself in
at regular intervals
to be subjected to (criticism)

to vote on (a law) / to be voted on
to become law
to control a passion
to meet an opponant
to abuse freedom / to be abused

to aim at (abolish)ing
to form one's own opinion
to act accordingly
anew = again
to be equal to

MEN AND MACHINES

When the Industrial Revolution came in the 19th century it completely changed the people's way of life. It was not a political revolution but a social change. Before this change, most people lived and worked in the country. When steam-power was discovered, the first steam-engines were used to drive machines. Factories were built and people left their villages to work in them. Big industrial towns sprang up and our modern way of life began. Since that time one new machine after another has been invented and changes have come thick and fast.

Machines have brought both advantages and disadvantages: more people have been employed since machines came in. The invention of the automobile (motor car), for instance, has created millions of jobs, not only for factory workers, but for service-station men, salesmen, roadmakers and many others.

Machines have relieved us of drudgery and have given us more free time. We need only think of the labour-saving devices that help the housewife - a refrigerator, for instance, a washing-machine, or a vacuum-cleaner.

In agriculture, too, the farmer is helped by many machines without which he could possibly not run his farm, as there is a shortage of farm-workers today. Houses and roads, too, could not be built so quickly without the help of machines.

Machines have made transport quicker and safer. Quick electric trains or jet planes take us to our destinations in a few hours. With the help of machines goods are mass-produced nowadays, so that they are cheap and available for all.

But machines have not only brought benefits, they have also brought disadvantages with them.

Industrialization has brought with it crowded cities, pollution of air and water and an unhealthy way of life. People do not take enough exercise and are always under the stress of modern life, so many get ill and die of heart attacks or other "manager's illnesses".

Industrialization sometimes brings mass unemployment. If factories produce too many goods or farmers raise too much wheat or cotton for the world market, they may find that they cannot sell at a profit. So the factory has to close down or the farmer lets some hired men go and many people lose their jobs.

Quick transport is sometimes a danger because small local wars can easily spread and become a danger to the whole world. Modern armies are equipped with terrible death-bringing machines and it is possible today for one aeroplane to drop a single bomb that can destroy a whole city with its millions of inhabitants.

Workers who stand at an assembly line in a factory do a monotonous job and only tend a machine. It is the machine that makes the article. So the machine has taken the joy and the pride out of work. Some artists have denounced the machine age as the death of art and skill.

In conclusion, I think that machines have made life easier and have given us more free time. It is the task of scientists and technicians to solve the problem of pollution and waste disposal that the machine age has brought us.

way of life
social change
to drive a machine
to spring up
thick and fast = in quick succession
to be employed
to create jobs / work
to relieve (someone) of = to take
  away
drudgery = the hardest work
to run a farm
a shortage of
mass-produced
to be available

pollution
to take exercise
to die of
mass unemployment
at a profit
to close down
to let (workers) go = to dismiss =
  to discharge
to become a danger to
to be equipped with
assembly line
to tend = to operate (a machine)
to denounce
waste disposal

MAN CONTENDING WITH NATURE

Ever since the beginnings of history, man has had to contend with the elements in his struggle for survival but he has also managed, with his superior intelligence, to subdue and harness them and put them to his own use. Early on, man realized the importance of fire without which he would doubtless have perished. Later on, after the wheel had been invented, water was used to turn primitive mills and people dug canals to irrigate dry land. Wind was used to drive sailing boats and to work water wheels. When the wheels turned, water was pumped to the surface. Great sailing boats were built and man braved the elements, crossed oceans and discovered new continents. When the New World was discovered the first settlers had to contend with great hardships. Not only were they attacked by hostile Indians, but they found it difficult to adapt themselves to a different climate. The first winter that the Pilgrim Fathers, for instance, experienced was terribly severe and about half their number died of cold, hunger and disease. But the rest managed to survive and to found a thriving colony.

Men are really very adaptable and ingenious and always seem to triumph over Nature in the end. But Nature gives them many difficult problems to solve. The Tennessee River, for example, regularly overflowed its banks and flooded the surrounding territory. Thousands of acres of land were made barren and the farmers became homeless and bankrupt. But during the Great Depression of the thirties the Federal Government under President Roosevelt financed the Tennessee Valley Authority in order to give employment to the workless. Over 20 dams were built which supply electricity to the surrounding countryside, valuable farmland was reclaimed and the farmers became prosperous. The course of the great river was regulated and now it never overflows its banks. It has also been dredged and is navigable for shipping.

The great St. Lawrence Seaway is another example of how man has harnessed a river to serve his own purposes. There is now a chain of canals connecting the St. Lawrence River with the Great Lakes, and the seaway is even navigable in winter.

The discovery of steam-power was a great step forward in man's struggle with Nature. Up to that time he had to rely on wind alone to drive ships across the ocean, and voyages in sailing ships were often hazardous and took a very long time if the wind was not favourable. But now steamships and oil- and atomic-driven ships cross the oceans rapidly and safely. Man has also harnessed water not only to supply electricity but to provide irrigation in dry lands. Man has learnt to fly and has even conquered space. In the year 1969 the first men landed on the moon.

But in spite of all these great achievements, man has not yet been able to prevent or contend with such natural disasters as earthquakes, hurricanes, avalanches or even great floods. In the case of hurricanes the population can be warned in time by meteorologists, but nobody can predict the exact time of an earthquake. Many floods have been caused by man's carelessness and irresponsibility. In his haste to conquer new continents and to acquire raw materials, man has ruthlessly cut down the forests. Now great tracts of country are eroded, rocky and barren.

In his novel "The Grapes of Wrath" John Steinbeck describes how a vast area of Oklahoma became a "dust bowl" because for decades the forests had been ruthlessly cut down. The land became so barren that the farmers were forced to leave and travel to the West, only finding work as ill-paid fruit-pickers.

This irresponsible denuding of forests has also led to dangerous floods, avalanches and landslides in recent years. The forests of Northern Italy were cut down ruthlessly throughout the centuries to provide wood for shipping and building. Then farmers built terraces of stone and cultivated the land. But during and after the Second

World War these farmers left to find work elsewhere and the terraces were neglected and gradually collapsed. After heavy rains a wave of flood water swept over Florence some years ago and did terrible damage. Many priceless art treasures were destroyed or damaged beyond repair. The same thing has happened in Austria in recent years so now experts have to solve the urgent problem of reforestation and the regulation of mountain streams and rivers.

In his hurry to achieve industrial prosperity, man has been heedless of the results of this development. It is only recently that people have realized the dangers of air and water pollution. Laws must now be passed to protect the population and to preserve wild life in reservations. When DDT was discovered it was used indiscriminately to spray great areas of cultivated land in order to kill insect pests. We have only recently realized that the indiscriminate use of insecticides is very dangerous. First, it can upset the balance of nature if all insects are destroyed and secondly, these insecticides contain poisonous substances which seep into the soil, poison the crops and cause great damage to the humans and animals that eat them.

Summing up, I think we can say that man has usually emerged triumphant from his struggle with Nature, but it has recently been discovered that his methods can have very dangerous side-effects. This problem can only be solved by teams of experts, working in international co-operation.

to contend with
to manage to = to succeed in (...ing)
to harness (the elements)
to put (something) to one's own use
to irrigate
to brave the elements
to adapt oneself to
to die of
adaptable
ingenious
to triumph over
to overflow its banks
to serve one's own purposes
a great step forward

to rely on = to depend on
to conquer space
in spite of
irresponsible, irresponsibly, irresponsibility
ruthless, ruthlessly, ruthlessness
beyond repair
to be heedless of
to preserve wild life
indiscriminate, indiscriminately
to upset the balance
to seep into
to cause damage to
to emerge triumphant
side-effects

WE LIVE IN A
CHANGING WORLD

"We live in a changing world" - how true this statement is today! We can actually witness changes during our lifetime - buildings are pulled down and new ones spring up around us, the face of the city changes, new machines are being invented every day. The Industrial Revolution in the 19th century was the beginning of this change caused by technology. Up to that time all countries were agricultural and only man- and animal-power, windpower and water-power had been used throughout the ages to transport people and goods and to run simple machines. But then steam-power was discovered to drive machines; great factories sprang up and also the railway came. These machines began to change life. People left their quiet country villages and flocked to the towns that began to grow up around the new factories. One great discovery or invention followed another in quick succession. Electric-power was discovered and electric light has today been brought to the most remote places. Steam trains are now being replaced by cleaner and smokeless electric trains. The oil-burning and the petrol-burning engines were invented and today life without motor-cars would be unthinkable.

The means of transport became quicker and safer, sailing boats were superseded by steamboats and later by oil-driven ships. Aeroplanes were invented that now carry people and goods rapidly from place to place, the journey taking only a few hours where formerly it took days, weeks or even months. Radio and telephone provide an easy and rapid means of communication between people all over the world. Life has become much quicker and more intense, although a higher standard of living has brought with it more leisure-time.

In recent years nuclear fission has been discovered and research scientists are working hard at developing atomic power and constructing space rockets and artificial satellites. Unfortunately, however, technical science has not only been devoted to improving our standard of living but also the construction of more and more terrible weapons. Through the rapid development of technical science and the improvement in methods of communication and transport, the world today has shrunk. Wars can no longer be confined and isolated; every war that begins in any part of the globe is a potential World War III.

Through gradual political reform or revolution, democracy has come to many countries. Education has been made general and social benefits such as health-insurance and old-age pensions guarantee a certain security to the people of the more advanced countries. The general trend of education towards independent thinking and acting has led to the breakdown of great colonial empires. Native people today are no longer willing to be held down by force, but wish to rule themselves. So the developing countries all over the world today are in a state of political ferment and change.

In this "changing world", in a time of political and technical change, the nations for the first time in history have begun to try to solve their problems at international conferences, united in their realization that only co-operation and mutual understanding will be able to avert the outbreak of a global war, some nuclear or other ecological catastrophe which could destroy all mankind.

to witness changes	to be devoted to (...ing)
to be pulled down	to shrink = to become smaller
to spring up	to be confined
throughout the ages	to be isolated
to flock to	to guarantee security
in quick succession	a trend towards
to be superseded by	a state of ferment and change
means of communication	mutual understanding
to bring with it	to avert = to prevent

MAN'S LEAP INTO SPACE

It is now many years since the first man, the Russian cosmonaut Juri Gagarin, was successfully launched into space (1961). His 108 minutes' stay in space proved conclusively that manned space flights were possible.
A great race between the U.S. on the one side, and the U.S.S.R. on the other was under way. It is therefore time now to pause for a moment and consider the question of space research. What has been achieved up to now?
Shortly before Apollo 11 was launched in 1969, Russian scientists sent an unmanned spaceship to the moon. Its probable mission was to land on the lunar surface, scoop up some soil and beat the Americans back to earth with the first samples of moon material. Luna 15, however, never achieved its goal, it dropped out of lunar orbit and probably crashed a few hours later after Armstrong and Aldrin became the first mortals to step on to the moon. Since then, other American lunar missions of the Apollo series have landed successfully on the moon. Between the December 1968 mission of Apollo 8 and the final flight of Apollo 17 in December 1972, a dozen U.S. astronauts walked on the lunar surface.
On the Apollo missions a huge rocket manned by three men was launched from the launch pad in Cape Kennedy.
The capsule sped on until it circled the moon. Two astronauts then climbed from the lunar command ship into the lunar module which separated from the mother ship and touched down on the moon. Meanwhile this mother ship continued to circle the moon. After spending some hours collecting samples of moon soil and rocks, erecting a seismometer and other apparatus, the astronauts returned into the lunar module, lifted off, linked up with the lunar command ship and climbed into it. The lunar module was ejected and the three men came back to earth.
After coming back into the earth's atmosphere the para-

chutes opened and the capsule sank slowly down in the air to splash down somewhere in the Pacific. A U.S. aircraft-carrier was waiting near, helicopters were at once sent which dropped frogmen into the sea. They helped the astronauts into boats from which they were hauled up into a helicopter and brought to the aircraft-carrier. On the first missions they had to spend some time in quarantine under medical supervision before they were allowed to return to their families and their work. Later, this quarantine was found to be unnecessary as the moon-dust contained no bacteria. The U.S. has now called off its programme of lunar exploration.

The Russians, however, have continued their experiments with unmanned spacecraft. In October 1970 Lunar 16 landed on the moon, gathered up a small sample of lunar soil, took off again and returned its cargo safely to the earth. Its landing operation on the Sea of Fertility, an unexplored portion of the moon about 200 miles east of Apollo 11's landing site, was controlled entirely by a computer programme fed from the earth - not by the combination of computers and manual controls used in Apollo lunar modules.

After the successful touchdown of Lunar 16, Lunar 17 was launched in November 1970. Three hours after reaching the moon aboard the mother ship, a strange machine, a robot called "Lunokhod I", moved off it and started to rove about the moon's surface under the direct control of TV monitors on earth. It was like a remote-controlled car, steered by solar cells that were charged when it opened its lid to the sunlight. It could move backwards and forwards, collect and analyse samples of lunar soil and report the findings to earth.

Only one month after the final visit of American astronauts to the moon, the Soviets successfully landed their second unmanned lunar rover in two years. Lunokhod II rolled down the gangplank of its lander and parked itself in a mountainous region, only about 100 miles from Apollo 17's Taurus-Littrow base. Under the direction of an earthbound "driver" the vehicle promptly began roving about the moonscape, sending back TV pictures to earth like its predecessor.

Another Soviet experiment was to launch a "parking" orbit - Salud. A few hours later three cosmonauts were launched in a Sojus capsule, linked up with the orbiting Salud for some hours, and then returned safely to earth. This seems to have been the first successful attempt at creating a space station and a space "shuttle". A joint U.S.-Soviet mission to create a space station took place in July, 1975.

The N.A.S.A. (National Aeronautics and Space Admini-

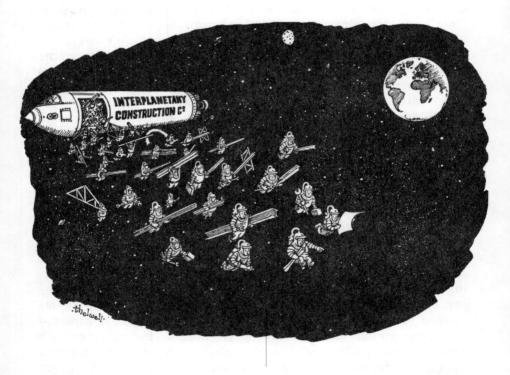

"Oh - about here, I should think....."   From PUNCH

stration) experts have already planned in detail various programmes. In one of these astronauts should have landed on Mars by the mid-1980s. In April 1985 the earth, Venus and Mars would have been in an ideal position for the mission. But this was called off for various reasons, mainly financial. They pushed on, however, with their space shuttle programme - a laboratory (skylab) in space and manned shuttle transportation to and fro.

On January 28th, 1986, the shuttle "Challenger" exploded at the blast-off, killing all six astronauts and one woman teacher aboard. This tragedy was a great shock to the American people and the whole shuttle programme has been put back several years. Now the Soviets seem to be leading in this particular field with their space station "Mir" and the development of a more sophisticated stronger rocket, Energia.

When considering the enormous progress made in the field of space research, one wonders if the vast expense and danger involved are justified. It is true that up to now fatal accidents have been comparatively rare but there seem to be far more pressing problems on earth waiting to be solved. Indeed, in the U.S., although the military authorities are very interested in developing spacecraft and continuing research, the budget of the N.A.S.A. has been drastically cut.

Many scientists, however, are enthusiastic and convinced that space research will contribute and has already contributed to earth technology in countless ways. For instance, the development of weather-satellites, TV satellites and computers would never have been achieved so quickly without the U.S. government's financial backing of NASA. NASA's research has also resulted in quieter jet engines, more efficient aircraft wings and improved air-traffic control. NASA may also contribute to improvement of earthly environment by solving such problems as pollution, waste elimination and the psychological effects of overcrowding. One scientist, even, assures us that there will not be another ice age - not

as long as we are moving ever further into the space age. There will be huge adjustable solar mirrors hung in space, many miles in diameter. Man won't have to suffer winters growing longer and colder; a wise use of orbiting space mirrors will solve that problem. One condition for the establishment of orbiting mirrors, of course, will be a functionating world government that will have to supervise and control their use.
Summing up, space research may lead to the co-operation of nations and may bring undreamed-of benefits to mankind as a whole.

to launch / to be launched into space
to prove conclusively
to be under way = to start
to scoop up = to collect
to drop out of orbit
launch pad
to speed on = to travel quickly
lunar command ship
lunar module
to touch down, a touchdown
samples, to collect samples, to analyse samples
to lift off
to link up with
to eject / to discard, to be ejected / to be discarded
to splash down, a splashdown
under medical supervision
to call off = to stop
landing site
to rove about = to move about

remote-control
space station
space shuttle
joint mission
to be blasted out of orbit
booster
to be lofted into orbit
to be latched = linked together
to kick out of orbit
to be retained = kept
to dock / to be docked
end to end
air locks
pressing = urgent (problems)
to be interested in (...ing)
to be cut = reduced
to contribute to
to result in
pollution
waste elimination
psychological effects of over-crowding
undreamed-of benefits

THE EMANCIPATION
OF WOMEN

Women's position in society has changed very much in the last 100 years. Until the 19th century a higher education was reserved for boys. Girls of the upper class were only taught needlework, a little painting, music and perhaps a foreign language. A girl was expected to stay at home and wait for a husband. When she got married all her dowry went to her husband, who could do with it what he liked. He was the sole authority in the family and responsible for the education of the children. There was little work an unmarried woman could do; she could work as a teacher, governess, dressmaker or in a factory, all for very little money. It was difficult, almost impossible, for a woman to go to a university, and women writers had to write under men's names.

Women realized that they must get the right to vote in order to change this situation. The first women to fight for voting rights in England, the Suffragettes, were very courageous and even aggressive. They went on hunger strike, hit policemen over the head with their umbrellas and were sent to prison. One suffragette was even killed when she tried to stop the Derby in protest against the unfair treatment of women.

At last World War I achieved what women had been vainly fighting for. As the men had to go to the front their places were taken by women. After the war men at last realized that industry could no longer function without the work of women. They were given the right to vote and their emancipation gradually began. The Franchise Act of 1918 gave the vote to all women over 30. Equal Franchise Act 1928 gave the vote to all persons over 21.

Nowadays, in most progressive countries, women have gained the same rights as men, being free to study at universities but not always earning equal payment for equal work. But in backward countries the situation of women is still very bad. In India, for example, there is still a high percentage of child marriages. Many girls become widows when they are still very young; but re-marriage and divorce are difficult for them.

Women are still considered as inferiors by the men who regard them as beasts of burden and child-bearing machines. In Africa most of the heavy agricultural labour is done by women, and also most of the trading in the food markets. In Moslem countries it is still very difficult for women to obtain a higher education, and even more difficult to have a career. Marriages are arranged by matchmakers and men regard their wives as their property and guard them jealously. A woman cannot go out unless she is accompanied by her husband or a female member of the family.

Even in enlightened countries there will never be absolute equality of the sexes because a married woman with a family and a profession has to do two jobs at the same time, while a man need only devote himself to his career. If a woman is single, I think we can say she has the same chances in life as a man. But the moment she marries, she must play a double role, not only working in her profession, but running her household as well. If she has children she must usually give up her job, unless she can afford to employ somebody to look after them.

Greater equality of the sexes might seem possible in a communist or other totalitarian regime where children are taken care of all day by the state. But even in such regimes the high-ranking women doctors, engineers and lawyers have to stand in queues at the shops with their lesser sisters after their work is done. They also have to look after their households, so they, too, are at a disadvantage.

Another attempt to achieve equality between men and women has been made in communes. Here several families live together under one roof and the men and the women take turns to do the cooking, shopping etc., and to look after the children. Although such experiments seem quite successful at first, one or the other member usually leaves the group and it finally breaks up. That can be very sad for the children, as the situation is even worse than in a divorce. When a group breaks up they lose their "brothers" and "sisters" and the other grownups, too.

Most of the working women today are unskilled workers in factories, typists, secretaries, shop assistants, nurses and hairdressers, while in the academic professions they are doctors and school teachers. Men still discriminate against them, however, in the higher professions and they have to fight hard against prejudice in order to gain a foothold in them.

"And for goodness sake try to be more masterful. C o m m a n d me to hand you the apron. C o m - m a n d me to get out of your kitchen!"

From PUNCH

In Austria today there are some, but very few, women judges, ambassadors and university professors. There are a few women politicians but not enough in proportion to the number of women in the country.

Top executive jobs are reserved for men, and women do not get the same chances of promotion. A top executive, for example, must be able to travel widely and a woman with a family cannot do this. If a woman is expecting a baby, her employer has to continue paying her salary for a time in her absence. She may not come back to work for a long time, so for this reason employers are unwilling to give high positions to women.

Men still have certain prejudices against women. They say they are unreliable and irrational; they make jokes, too, about women's driving abilities and claim that they are not even capable of thinking clearly. Women retort that men are afraid of real competition; they cling to their supremacy because of a basic inferiority complex.

Summing up, women have shown that they are not merely objects of pleasure for men and that they are capable of holding high positions. But they are always at a disadvantage if they have to combine a job and a family.

In backward countries very much has to be done for the emancipation of women. Until they are allowed to have an education and the same rights as men there will never be real equality of the sexes.

to be reserved for
to be expected to
dowry
the right to vote
to go on hunger strike
to be sent to prison
in protest against
vainly = in vain = unsuccessfully
to gain the same rights as '
to be considered as inferiors
beasts of burden
child-bearing machines
equality of the sexes
to devote oneself to
the moment (she marries) = as
    soon as

to play a double role
high-ranking
to stand in a queue
to be at a disadvantage
to take turns to
unskilled workers
to discriminate against
to gain a foothold
in proportion to
top executive jobs / a top exe-
    cutive
to be capable of (...ing)
to retort = to answer angrily
to cling to
inferiority complex
merely = only
objects of pleasure

THE DEVELOPMENT OF SOCIETY

Science and technology have brought enormous changes to society in the course of the last decades. Technology has brought time- and labour-saving machines which give people more leisure time and free them of drudgery.
Communications and transport have been made quicker and easier, and medical science has made enormous progress in stamping out diseases which were formerly fatal and in raising the general standard of world health.
But when discussing the question of what has improved human society in the course of time, it is far better to disregard the subject of technical progress - which, after all, has also brought with it certain problems and disadvantages - and to examine the change in human ideas.
One of the most important changes is the general spreading of the idea of the equality of mankind. This idea has also been preached by various religions and political groups and is contained in the American Declaration of Independence, but it has never really been put into action until the present day. In the past there were always conquered peoples and slaves who had to work for their masters. The European powers had colonies

I wanted to save time, but in any case the insurance will pay.....

overseas and the white people considered themselves as a "master race". Society itself had strong class barriers and was divided into upper class or aristocracy, middle class and "working class". But today these barriers are falling or have already fallen. In most countries people have the right to vote and the right to a good education. In many countries, too, women have been able to achieve equal rights with men. The former colonies have become independent and govern themselves. Coloured people are no longer willing to be ruled or exploited. In the United States, where the blacks have always been considered in the Southern States as inferior beings, the Civil Rights Act is at last changing this state of affairs and is forcing the "segregationist" whites to give the coloured people equal rights. This is one of the most important ways in which society has improved in the course of time.

Another change is to be seen in the development of a social conscience. In former times, when society was mainly agricultural, problems such as unemployment, old age and the care of the sick did not arise. Families lived together on the land; there was plenty of work for everyone, and if a member of the family was old or helpless he was cared for by the others. But the Industrial Revolution changed all this: people who are themselves badly housed and badly paid cannot care for their poorer and older relatives. Something had to be done to help these people. The work of private charities was not enough and it became clear that the state must take on the responsibility for the care of old people, the sick, the unemployed and the destitute. Gradually the trade unions, which tried to obtain better conditions for the working man, arose in all European countries. At the same time the various political parties made it a part of their programme to bring in various social reforms such as factory inspection, health insurance and old-age pensions. The state has not only been forced to take on the responsibility of dealing with such problems as poverty and sickness, but also of providing housing for the poor. In the 19th century during the Industrial Revolution unscrupulous speculators built houses quickly for the rapidly increasing industrial population; these were badly built, unhealthy dwellings which became terrible slums. The responsibility for building homes for the working population has therefore gradually fallen on the local authorities who now erect healthy flats, full of sun and air. A system of unemployment insurance now exists in most countries, too, by which workers pay a small amount of their wages as insurance, and are then supported by the state if they lose their jobs.

Thus social insecurity has today been largely banished in Europe, though by no means all over the world.

The idea of a social conscience, that people are responsible for the welfare of their under-privileged fellows, is taking root. This idea has spread to world politics.

In order to prevent a repetition of the chaos and economic breakdown which was the result of World War I, the U.S. poured money into the vanquished states of Europe after World War II to help their recovery. Politicians today realize that poverty is a breeding-ground for anarchy and political unrest and so the under-developed countries of Asia and Africa are helped by means of financial and educational aid programmes.

The growth of the idea of world brotherhood is one of the most important recent developments of human society.

The threat of atomic war and also of the destruction of all life on our planet through the greenhouse effect hangs over all nations alike, and so the statesmen of the world realize that our only chance of survival is in peaceful discussion of our problems and in constructive co-operation for a better world.

in the course of (time)
technology / technical progress /
    technical science
time-saving
labour-saving
to free (someone) of
drudgery = the hardest work
to make progress in (...ing)
to stamp out (diseases)

to disregard = to pay no attention
    to
to preach (an idea)
to put into action = to carry out
to consider oneself as / to be con-
    sidered as
social conscience
to care for / to be cared for
to be badly housed

to be badly paid
to take on the responsibility for
    (something) / of (...ing)
to make it part of one's programme
to bring in (reforms)
to deal with (a problem)
to provide (something) for (some-
    one) / (someone) with (something)
local authorities

unemployment insurance
social insecurity
to banish = to get rid of
by no means = not
under-privileged
to take root
breeding-grounds for / of (anarchy,
    etc.)
alike = in the same way

T R A V E L   B R O A D E N S
T H E   M I N D

Travel is easy and comparatively cheap today. Through
modern means of transport - motor car, plane, railway,
steamship - the world has shrunk. Travel has become
popular among all classes of the population, even those
who are not so well-to-do can afford nowadays to go
on charter flights and take part in package tours.

Whether travel broadens the mind, however, depends
largely on the way in which a person travels. (Compare
quick round tours with an extended stay in a foreign
place; in the former you are hurried around the princi-
pal places of interest in a group by a guide, you stay
only at special tourist hotels, eat only in certain restaurants, etc.; in the latter you have time to stroll around,
to get to know the inhabitants, and to absorb the atmosphere.)
In former centuries it was part of a nobleman's education to travel, to make the Grand Tour, visiting all the
important European capitals and places of interest, before he settled down at home. Today it is also the fashion for students and young people in general to travel
as much as possible in the vacation. But the style of
travel has changed very much in the years since the
war. Nowadays the young people travel from place to
place, carrying only a rucksack with a bedroll and few
clothes; they are members of an enormous international army of travellers. They do not go to the usual

famous cities, but prefer out-of-the-way and picturesque places. They travel thousands of miles in order to attend a pop-festival on the Isle of Wight, Great Britain, for example, or a bull-fighting festival at Pamplona, Spain. On their travels they must meet many different people and have many strange adventures. All this will give them a broad-minded outlook on life.

Many writers have drawn their inspiration from travel and life abroad. Among modern novelists who did so I can mention Ernest Hemingway and Somerset Maugham. Hemingway wrote of fishermen in the Gulf of Mexiko, of bull-fighters in Spain and big-game hunters in Africa. Somerset Maugham wrote of Englishmen living in the colonies, in Malaya and the South Sea Islands.

Travelling abroad gives us an opportunity to learn or perfect our knowledge of foreign languages. We learn English at school, but to speak fluently and perfectly it would be essential to travel to England or America. There are various student organizations which facilitate student exchange programmes. Trips at reduced rates are arranged, and places for foreign students are found in English or American families.

A good knowledge of English is very important as it is one of the main languages spoken in the world today. It is spoken in Africa, India, Pakistan, etc., where there are hundreds of different native dialects; it is spoken at international conferences; it is the language of air-control at all international airports, and it is used in scientific publications and for the texts of most pop and beat music.

Young people have the opportunity nowadays to go to the developing countries as volunteer workers. Working on the spot in these countries, they get to know the problems of the people who live there.

Summing up, I can say that no matter whether travel is undertaken for pleasure, for education or in order to help the people of the developing countries, it certainly broadens the mind.

to shrink = to become smaller
to become popular among
well-to-do
charter flight
package tour
to broaden the mind
..., however, ... = But
to depend on
an extended stay = a long stay
the former... the latter...
to be the fashion for (someone) to
to hitch-hike

out-of-the-way
a broad-minded outlook on life

to perfect one's knowledge of
to facilitate = to make easy
at reduced rates
air-control
scientific publications
on the spot
to get to know
to undertake (travel) / to be undertaken

V I O L E N C E

Violence has long been used for political motives. All through history we can find examples of people rising in rebellion to overthrow a tyrant or a system of government (the murder of Julius Caesar, the French Revolution). Indeed, the much admired American form of government found its beginnings in a bloody revolution and war against the British. Similarly, the British parliamentary system developed in the course of a long and bitter struggle between the king and Parliament to decide who should be supreme: Magna Charta 1215, the Civil War 1642-48, the Bloodless Revolution 1688.
Other countries, like France and Russia, have had violent and more terrible revolutions, and a wave of anarchy swept across the globe before the First World War. At that time the President MacKinley of America and Empress Elizabeth of Austria were assassinated.
At the present time there is a great spread of urban violence and terrorism. "The street is the stage", said one American terrorist; and in cities throughout the world that stage is alive with alarming activities; politically motivated arson, bombing, kidnapping or murder. The terrorist activity is world-wide, and most of it is carried out by a new type in the history of political warfare: the urban guerilla.
One form of terrorism has usually been caused originally by oppression. In an undemocratic country all opposition

is ruthlessly oppressed, and the opponents of the regime are imprisoned, tortured and even killed. So the only method of opposing the regime is by political blackmail. Groups of extreme radicals kidnap foreign diplomats or businessmen in order to force their governments to free political prisoners. In this case some sympathy can be felt for their cause, although their means are not justified.

Then there are political fanatics who hi-jack planes either in order to reach inaccessible countries like Cuba or North Korea themselves or to force foreign governments to release imprisoned terrorists (e.g., P.L.O. terrorists) who have been justly tried and sentenced. These actions are criminal because quite innocent people suffer and are endangered.

In other cases of hi-jacking people try to escape from totalitarian states by forcing the aeroplane pilot to change course and land in a democratic country. As this is their only means of escape, we cannot help feeling sympathy for such desperate people.

Oppressed people often turn to violence. In North America, for instance, the blacks have long felt that they have been unfairly treated and this feeling finds expression in rioting and urban violence. A militant black group called the Black Panthers was formed during the sixties. At that time, too, some extreme left-wing white students in the U.S. formed a group, calling themselves the Weather Men, to protest against the Vietnam War and American supremacy in the world, aiming to shock and frighten society, "the Establishment", by bombing well-known companies such as IBM, Mobil and General Telephone in New York. They even exploded a bomb in the Capitol Building in Washington. A similar group, the Baader-Meinhof "gang", has been active in Western Germany for several years.

What do these terrorists want? Their ideologies differ but in general the aim is to destroy what cannot be reformed. They think that "the system" is incapable of real change and that the official violence of the government (police, prisons, army) can only be counteracted by more violence. They all share the spirit of anarchism, its love of violence, its chaotic organization, its insistence on absolute freedom (an illusion that in the past has always led to tyranny.)

The present spread of terrorism is a result of technology's multiplication of the power to destroy. Instant communications guarantee a global spread of radicalism. Organizations like the Black Panthers in the U.S., the I.R.A. in Ireland and the Palestinian guerillas exchange not only ideas and moral support, but also financial backing.
What is the solution? Defeat over terror is of little benefit if it leads to a police force with permanently enlarged powers and a population with permanently curtailed rights. In fact, this is precisely what many of the guerillas want to bring about - government repression that provokes widespread discontent and ultimately - revolution. The final weapon against the urban guerilla is a secure and self-confident society that can contain its enemies without resorting to the terrorists' own methods.

to rise in rebellion
to overthrow
to find its beginnings in
in the course of
to be assassinated
urban (violence, terrorism,
    guerilla)
politically motivated
to oppress = to crush
to oppose, opposition, opponent
political blackmail
to feel sympathy for
cause
to be justified
to hi-jack
to release = to set free
to be tried
to be sentenced

to change course
to turn to (violence, crime)
to find expression in
to protest against
the Establishment
to be counteracted by
to share = to have in common
insistence on
multiplication = increase = en-
    largement
instant = rapid
support = backing
to be of benefit
permanently enlarged
permanently curtailed = reduced
to bring about
to contain = to control
to resort to = to employ

PERSONALITIES WHO HAVE SERVED WORLD PEACE

One of the first personalities to serve the cause of world peace was Alfred Nobel (1833-1896), the Swedish chemist and industrialist. He invented various explosives, including dynamite, thus furthering the development of munitions which have brought great misery to mankind. Realizing what he had done, he tried to atone for it by leaving the interest on his immense fortune (about DM 150.000) to the Nobel Prize Foundation. Since 1901 this prize has been awarded every year for great achievements in the field of physics, chemistry, medicine, literature and the peace movement. By encouraging people to work for international peace and by rewarding them for their work in this field, Alfred Nobel has done much to further this cause.

The first man to win the Nobel Peace Prize in 1901 was Henri Dunant, a Geneva banker (1828-1910). He conceived the idea of an International Red Cross movement on the battlefield of Solferino in 1859. His hatred of war was awakened in the midst of the suffering of the severely wounded. On the battlefield he realized that there was a wonderful chance of saving many of the wounded and of mitigating the inhumanity of war by an internationally protected organization of trained helpers. In his book "Memories of Solferino" Dunant described how he had found 40,000 dead and wounded on the battlefield. He saw severely wounded Austrians, who were lying amongst French and Italians, being thrown out of the church of Castiglione. He sprang on the steps of the church and cried out, "Don't do it! Tutti fratelli, all brothers!" Inspired by Dunant, Italian students, Austrian doctors, an Italian priest, a French reporter, Swiss, English and the women of the village now nursed the wounded Italians, French, Austrians, Croats, Hungarians and Poles without discrimination.

Dunant sent 1,600 copies of his book with accompanying letters to all the courts of Europe, to ministries and newspaper editors, demanding an international and legally binding agreement which, after being established and signed, could serve as the basis for the foundation of societies to aid the wounded in different countries.

He travelled about to the different governments, gave lectures, sent letters of appeal, not thinking of his own business nor of the enormous amount of money that this publicity cost. In October, 1863, 26 representatives from 17 countries agreed to found auxiliary societies, having as their symbol a red cross on a white background.

On August 22, 1864 the government representatives of 12 nations signed the famous Geneva Convention, thus founding the International Red Cross. From now on all field and military hospitals with their staffs were to be recognized as neutral and protected; this example was followed by nearly all countries.

Dunant was at first overwhelmed with honours, but was soon neglected and forgotten when he went bankrupt on account of his idealistic work. He lived on in poverty and misery until he was found again by a friend in 1889. The conscience of the world was now awakened and an effort was made to make good the wrong done to him. He was awarded the first Nobel Peace Prize in 1901 and used the sum to satisfy his creditors, donating the rest to charity. Dunant's work continued to develop after his death. Today the International Red Cross includes over 60 national societies, the International Committee at Geneva and the Paris League of Red Cross Societies. The Swiss International Committee forms an impartial link between nations at war, tries to find missing soldiers, inspects prisoner-of-war camps and also helps in peacetime in the event of disasters such as earthquakes or floods and in refugee camps.

Millions of men and women work voluntarily for this organization, alleviating by their work the suffering of mankind.

In 1953 the Nobel Peace Prize was awarded to Albert

Schweitzer. Doctor Schweitzer was a theologian, doctor, university professor, organist and authority on Bach. He has been a model of inspiration to all those working for true peace among nations. Since 1913 he devoted his life to helping the African natives in his hospital at Lambarene in the Congo (near Gabun). By his example he showed that it is possible to live an unselfish life in the service of humanity.

The American George Catlett Marshall (1880-1959), who shared the Nobel Peace Prize with Albert Schweitzer in 1953, did very much for the peace in the world. After having been Chief of the General Staff during World War II he was American Foreign Secretary from 1947-1949. During that time he conceived the Marshall Plan, a brilliant scheme to help the post-war recovery of the European nations. Knowing from experience, from the time of the First World War, that financially ruined nations are a prey to inflation and political unrest and revolution, he instituted a large-scale plan (known later as the European Recovery Programme, E.R.P.) by which the nations of Europe were generously aided by the U.S. government. They were supplied with goods from the U.S., but instead of paying the U.S. suppliers direct, the European recipients paid into a fund which was then used to supply loans to build up their industries. This programme is still continuing its work today, supplying industrial enterprises and projects with loans at a lower rate of interest than the banks demand. Through the Marshall Plan European recovery from the effects of war has been very rapid and with trade booming, the standard of living is higher than ever before. Owing to George Marshall's far-sightedness an economic situation, such as there was in Europe after 1918, was prevented. By his plan he did much to avert the danger of a future war.

These personalities should be an example and an inspiration to all those who hate war and who wish to work for international peace.

to serve the cause of (peace)
thus = in this way
to bring misery to
to atone for
the interest on (a fortune, capital)
to award a prize / to be awarded
to reward (someone) for
to conceive (an idea, a plan)
in the midst of
a chance of (...ing)
without discrimination
to serve as the basis for
to give lectures
letter of appeal
auxiliary society

to be overwhelmed with = covered
    with
to go bankrupt
on account of = because of
to make good
prisoner-of-war camp
to alleviate = to relieve (suffe-
    ring, misery)
to devote one's life to (...ing)
post-war recovery
from experience
to be a prey to = to suffer from
to supply, to be supplied with
at a (low, high) rate of interest
to boom
far-sightedness
to avert = to prevent

I D E A L I S M

Do the young people of today still have ideals?
Before discussing this question, one must first define the word "ideal". It can either mean a person who has set an example to be emulated, or some aim one tries to attain. I think it is much more difficult for the youth of today to have the latter type of ideal than in former times. They have been disillusioned by two world wars and they have seen how political ideals have been betrayed and corrupted. Before the First and the Second World Wars the young people were inspired by nationalistic ideals, but now realize to what a terrible disaster this can lead. Before the evils of a Communist dictatorship were exposed, many young people in different countries were inspired by the ideal of a classless society. Thousands of them, for instance, out of sheer idealism, volunteered to fight in the International Brigade in the Spanish Civil War. But they were defeated and betrayed, sometimes by their own comrades. Now they know that a classless society is an impossible utopia and not worth fighting for. Many young people, too, were formerly inspired by religious ideals, but they also seem to have become sceptical and disillusioned.

-70-

In England, particularly in the 'twenties and 'thirties, the plight of the unemployed was so terrible that idealists and reformers were inspired to achieve by degrees the Welfare State, which now guarantees social security from the cradle to the grave. But the younger generation of the working class, having attained a comparatively high standard of living, is no longer interested in the old political problems.

There are still, however, some fanatical idealists today who perform acts of extraordinary courage and selflessness. (I am thinking of the Buddhist monks of Vietnam who poured petrol over themselves and set fire to it as a protest against a corrupt regime. Jan Pallach, a young Czechoslovakian idealist also committed suicide in this way as a protest against the Russian occupation of his country in 1968.)

But these are isolated examples of an exalted idealism, and in these days of ruthless power politics they have not achieved much success. It is, perhaps, only by following an ideal in a constructive and consistent way that some great aim can be achieved.

Mahatma Gandhi is an example of a great idealist. He preached a policy of non-violence and a total boykott of British goods in order to achieve his aim: the independence of India. He was imprisoned many times by the British but at last he achieved his aim only by peaceful means.

Martin Luther King, the American black leader, also preached non-violence to attain his aim: equal rights for the blacks in America. It is ironical that both these peaceful idealists were assassinated by ruthless fanatics. Although the ideals Gandhi and King fought for (independence of colonies and equal rights for all men) still hold good, it is not surprising that the youth of today is disillusioned. So many colonies have won their independence, only to be torn by inner strife between warring tribes and ruled by corrupt politicians, that they are sometimes in a worse state than under a benevolent colonial administration. Those fighting for equal rights for coloured people have also become discouraged because the situation seems to be getting worse instead of better. The blacks in America have become embittered by their long wait for justice and many now resort to violence and vandalism. This gives the fanatic white racialists an excuse to resort to violence, too.

Many young people confuse ideals with idols. An idol is worshipped with exaggerated reverence which, however, is only superficial and shortlived. Pop-singers, beat-groups like the Beatles or the Rolling Stones, sportsmen and film-stars are surrounded by enormous publicity and admired by countless young people. They listen reverently to all the gossip about their idols and copy their dress and mannerisms. But this admiration, as I said before, is only short-lived and constitutes a phase through which young people pass. They do not admire their idols because of their characters or private lives, but only because of their achievements in the fields of music, acting or sport.

A real ideal to be admired should have an exemplary character and should, in my opinion, benefit mankind in some way. Albert Schweitzer perhaps is one of these. He gave up everything to go and live in the African jungle where he founded a hospital and devoted his life to caring for the sick. Henri Dunant in the last century also devoted his life to an ideal. Horrified by the sufferings of the wounded after the Battle of Solferino, he conceived the idea of an international organization to relieve the sufferings of the wounded soldiers and prisoners of war. Without the aid of the Red Cross many thousands would doubtless have perished in and after the last two world wars. The Red Cross also helps the stricken populations of the world in times of national disaster, after floods, earthquakes and hurricanes. There is another idealist in our time, Herbert Gmeiner, who has devoted his life to founding children's villages all over the world. In these villages orphaned children are cared for and brought up in a family atmosphere and lead happy normal lives. There are also countless unknown idealists all over the world, working as doctors, nurses, teachers and missionaries, offering their services to build up the industry and welfare institutions of the developing countries.

In conclusion, I think one can say that there is still room for ideals, even in our modern materialistic society, and there are still idealists who devote themselves to good causes. Much work remains to be done, for instance, for drug addicts, the disabled and the mentally sick. Beside aid from the state, individuals can really help such people by their genuine interest and identification with their problems. Other idealists fight to save animals from cruelty and extinction and to protect our environment by joining organisations like Greenpeace or the World Wildlife Fund.

On the other hand, young people of today should not be blamed too much if they tend to be sceptical and disillusioned in view of the present state of the world.

to emulate (an example), to be
  emulated
to attain = to achieve (an aim, an
  end
to be / to become disillusioned
to expose (evils) = to show up
to be inspired by
to be (not) worth (...ing)
to guarantee (social security)
..., however, ... = But
ruthless power politics
a policy of non-violence
a total boycott
by peaceful means
to be assassinated
to hold good = to be valid
to be torn by inner strife
to become discouraged, disillusioned,
  embittered
to resort to = to turn to (violence,
  vandalism)

to confuse ... with
to be worshipped = loved = admired
exaggerated = very great (reverence)
surrounded by publicity
to constitute = to consist of
an exemplary character
to relieve (suffering)
doubtless = no doubt = certainly
to perish = to die
stricken population
to be cared for
to be brought up
a good cause
to volunteer, to work as a
  volunteer
to be blamed
to tend to
in view of = considering

HEROES AND HEROISM

Let us begin with the definition of a hero: an extremely brave person or one who risks his life to save others. The question that confronts us is whether there are still "heroes" today.

The heroes of antiquity, Jason, Hercules, etc., were demigods endowed with almost superhuman powers in their struggles against their enemies. The great military leaders throughout the ages, Alexander, Julius Caesar, Napoleon, Washington or Wellington are still regarded by their respective countries as heroes, even though their actions may have plunged others into untold misery. In those days the maxim "Right or wrong my country" still held, so nobody questioned whether their courage was admirable or not.

Today, I think, one considers a hero as someone to be emulated, whose actions have a beneficial effect either on another person or on mankind as a whole.

Bernard Shaw satirizes heroism in his play "Arms and the Man". The romantic heroic officer Sergius who led a cavalry charge against an enemy armed with cannons is shown up to be a stupid fellow. His deed is suicidal, or rather would have been if the enemy had not had the wrong munition.

There are still, of course, opportunities of showing great personal courage in a modern war, but war itself has become a dirty and immoral business, no longer confined to the battlefield. In my opinion the heroes of today are those who show moral courage or who act courageously, without hesitating, in the emergencies of everyday life.

In his short story "The Door of Opportunity" Somerset Maugham describes a refined and conceited District Officer in the colonies, who, when the manager of a neighbouring rubber plantation is murdered by rebellious Chinese coolies, hesitates before setting out to rescue the planter's half-caste wife and children. He makes a careful plan of action and waits some days until he has got enough police reinforcements before venturing into the jungle to the plantation. When he arrives there with his policemen, he finds that a choleric Dutchman, living on a nearby plantation, has long since rushed there, accompanied by only one native assistant, quelled the rebellion and saved the murdered man's family. This Dutchman is rather an ignorant, crude man but extremely courageous because he acted without hesitating, as a matter of course, with no thought of the danger to himself.

A similar situation is described in Joseph Conrad's "Lord Jim". The cowardly white crew, including Lord Jim, jump into the life boats, and they row away in the darkness, leaving their ship, which is crowded with sleeping Indian pilgrims, to its fate. The ship has struck some object in the Indian ocean but does not sink at all. Some time later the French captain of a passing ship, coming across the abandoned vessel, at great danger to himself, boards it, takes it in tow and brings it safely into harbour. This he does without hesitating, it is his duty and therefore a matter of course. Another rather stolid and ordinary seaman, Captain MacWhirr, is described in Conrad's story "Typhoon". He steers his ship safely through the most terrible storm and keeps the terrified Chinese passengers from flying at one another's throats when their chests, which contain the silver dollars that they have saved and are taking home, burst open. He keeps his head, saves the ship and at the end of the voyage prevents a massacre among the coolies by distributing the money evenly to them.

Of course the two seamen described here are types who have been trained for such work and it can be said that they are only doing their duty. Policemen, firemen, lighthousemen and mountain rescue teams belong to this category. We take it for granted that they risk their lives as all part of their day's work; nevertheless, to my mind, some of them are heroes.

We read almost every day in the newspaper of brave deeds. There are people who jump into the water to save others from drowning, passers-by who overwhelm armed and dangerous criminals, people who rush into burning houses to save others, and so on. These people have not been specially selected and trained for dangerous work, like the astronauts are, but they behave like heroes when some emergency arises.

Besides those who save the lives of others in a spectacular way, there are the quiet heroes we never hear much about. I am thinking, for instance, of doctors working in laboratories and experimenting on themselves to find the cure to some terrible diseases. We should not forget to mention, either, those people who put up a terrific struggle against illness and disability, and in spite of being blind, paralysed or having lost their limbs, do not give way to despair and manage to live cheerful and useful lives.

People who show moral courage also rank among the heroes of today. Our times are just as cruel and dangerous as the dark ages of history. All over the world there are brutal dictatorships, military and communist, where all opposition is ruthlessly crushed. In such countries to stand up and state one's views without fear is an act of great heroism. Even the writers are punished if they deviate from the party line. Many are still languishing in prisons, in labour camps, or in mental homes. Yet some free citizens are not afraid to speak out for their collegues.

So in conclusion I think we can say that heroism has not died out but our conception of it has perhaps changed in the course of time.

```
to be endowed with
to be regarded as
to plunge (someone) into misery
to be emulated
beneficial = helpful = good
to be shown up = to be exposed
to be confined to
without hesitating, withour hesi-
    tation
emergency
to quell = to subdue (a rebellion)
```

```
as a matter of course
cowardly
to leave (the ship) to its fate
to come across = to find by chance
a great danger to oneself
to keep (someone) from ...ing =
    to prevent from
to keep one's head
to do one's duty
to take it for granted
all part of one's day's work
```

to put up a struggle against
in spite of (... ing)
to give way to (despair)
to manage to = to succeed in
(... ing)
to rank among = to take one's
place among
to be ruthlessly crushed =
oppressed

to state one's views
to deviate from the party line
to languish = to lose health and
strength
to be confined to (a mental home)
And yet = But
to die out
in the course of time

CRIME AND PUNISHMENT

When writing on this theme it is important to say something about the causes of crime. There are two schools
of thought on this: the first that people become criminals on account of the evil influence of their surroun-
dings, the second is that the criminal instinct is some
kind of organic failing and is hereditary.
In recent years there has been a sharp increase in juvenile delinquency. It must, therefore, to some extent
be due to the permissive and affluent society in which
we live. It is not only the underprivileged children who
become criminals but often those of well-to-do parents.
These, both father and mother, are occupied in earning
money while the "latch-key" children have to fend for
themselves. Influenced by the brutality shown on cinema
and TV screen their idols may be gangsters or supermen
of the James Bond type. In the materialistic outlook
of the affluent society there is also a general decline
in religious faith and morals.
Once caught and convicted, a juvenile in prison can
become influenced by fellow-prisoners and drift deeper
into crime on his release. Among the inmates of prison
the "professional criminal" is the type that prevails. With
few exceptions members of this group have graduated
from "approved schools" and "borstals". In his teens the
professional has chosen crime as a career because he
believes it will provide him with "plenty of money without working for it". Finding the world a jungle, he brands

all honest men as "hypocrites" who simply lack the courage of their desires. Professional criminals gaze with a kind of malicious envy on the world with its material wealth. The purpose of society, they believe, is nothing more than the acquisition of goods by any means. Religion and law are only "tricks" by means of which the rich and powerful establish empire over the poor and weak. Material success is the only morality. In schools, business, industry, in society everywhere the cry is - get rich! Be a top person! Look after yourself and yours! So they see nothing wrong in getting their share of affluence from the community by any method. They refute the idea that imprisonment acts in any way as an expiation because none of them claims to feel the slightest guilt.

A second type of criminal is the one who chooses crime not as a way of life but as a profitable sideline. These part-time crooks, like their professional colleagues, remain utterly convinced that, given the certainty of not being found out, all men are dishonest and that honesty is strictly for "mugs", (a person who is innocent and may be easily deceived.)

Among criminals there are many who are undersized dullards. These physically deprived, objects of indifference, ridicule or contempt, prove their importance to society by breaking its laws. By doing so they work off their basic inferiority-complexes.

In the prison system there are also two broad schools of thought constantly at odds with each other. The "free-willers", following Christian doctrine, believe in the ability of the individual to choose between good and evil, and in the need to punish, to reform, and finally forgive those who have made the wrong decision. The "determinists" maintain that a man's field of choice has been severely restricted by heredity and environment and that every delinquent is a victim of circumstances. Neither punishment nor forgiveness, they believe, is necessary for his rehabilitation; only his habits and attitudes need to be thoroughly retrained so that he may fit better into a free, tolerant society. The first school, now long established in power, has failed badly in keeping the persistent delinquent out of prison. It remains to be seen whether the new reformers will be any more successful. In order to achieve their ends they must first solve the problems of the lack of personnel and suitable prison buildings.

Since World War II the reformers have succeeded in abolishing the death penalty in most Western countries. But in recent years the pattern of crime has changed. There has been a sharp increase in crimes of violence - armed robbery, kidnapping, terrorism and hi-jacking. So the call for the reintroduction of capital punishment for certain crimes has been heard in many places. Many people in Great Britain, for instance, think that hanging should be brought back for the killing of children and policemen, for murder committed during armed robbery or for brutal acts of terrorism.

Dostoyevsky, in "The Idiot", put the case against capital punishment very eloquently. Prince Myshkin says:

"Yet the worst pain is perhaps not inflicted by wounds, but by knowledge that in an hour, in ten minutes, in half a minute, now, this moment your soul will fly out of your body, and that you will be a human being no longer, and that that's certain .... Just when you lay your head under the knife and you hear the swish of the knife as it slides down over your head - it is just that fraction of a second that is the most awful of all .... To kill for murder is an unmeasurably greater evil than the crime itself. Murder by legal process is unmeasurably more dreadful than murder by a brigand."

He goes on to say that a man killed by brigands at night in a forest still hopes up to the last moment that he will be saved. Or a soldier fired at in battle will still hope, but if he is read his death sentence he will go mad or burst out crying. These arguments are certainly true, but the victim of a sadistic sex murderer or a hostage held by a desperate terrorist must suffer the same agonies before an almost certain death.

It seems that capital punishment should perhaps be re-introduced to act as a deterrent against certain crimes, and not least to protect society from criminals who will murder again once they are released.

Summing up, we can say that the purpose of law, punishment and correction is to protect society from the criminal. But research into the causes of crime should be continued so that the punishment of criminals in the future will be more preventive than repressive.

schools of thought
on account of = because cf
a sharp increase in
juvenile delinquency = juvenile
    crime
to some extent
to be due to = to be caused by
permissive society
affluent society
underprivileged children
latch-key children
to fend for oneself
approved school = borstal (school
    for juvenile delinquents)

to lack the courage of one's de-
    sires
to refute = to prove as wrong
to work off (a complex, aggression)
to be at odds with = to quarrel
    with
field of choice
a victim of circumstances
the persistent delinquent, criminal
it remains to be seen
to hold (someone) as hostage
to act as a deterrent
preventive
repressive

"What about prison?
I think, life cannot be better!"

Franz Hrastnik (1958) in
    "Opernkonserve"

SOURCES OF ENERGY

The present world-wide demand for energy has been caused by the increase in the world population, and the consequent spread of industrialization, which in its turn has brought with it the mechanization of offices, agriculture, mining, transport, communications, and also of households. Fuel reserves are dwindling and so the question as to whether our present sources of energy will be able to meet the demands of the future must be solved.

What are the power resources that we have at our disposal today?

At the turn of the century   c o a l   was the most important source of energy. The coal-producing countries Great Britain and the United States were the first countries to become highly industrialized. Coal reserves will not be fully exhausted for the next 5000 years. Meanwhile, concern for the environment has made coal unpopular with the ecologists, though energy experts claim that it still has an important future.

O i l   - a finite fossil fuel like coal - has been its greatest rival since the middle of the 20th century. Within 40 years, according to some estimates, oil supplies will have run out - optimists put the figure at 100 years. The main oil producing areas are the Middle East, U.S., the Caribbean and U.S.S.R. Lately, however, great oil deposits, belonging to Great Britain and Norway, have been found in the North Sea. The work of drilling from oil rigs in the sea is both dangerous and expensive. Gushers, like the one caused by a blow-out on a Norwegian oil rig in 1977, can cause extensive damage to the environment. The oil and petroleum exporting countries (OPEC) have combined to control prices and also to limit the production of oil as the reserves are not infinite.

The exploitation of   w a t e r   p o w e r   is of ancient origin. The large hydro-electric power plants of today serve multiple purposes: the production of electric power, the regulation of rivers, artificial irrigation, et cetera. Electric energy is obtained from generators driven by water turbines. The source of water may be natural (waterfall) or artificial (river-damming). The coming of hydro-electric power has had great importance for the location of industry. Before, factories had to be built near coal-mines, the source of fuel supply, and so industry was concentrated in certain parts of the country. Now the cables bring power to wherever it is wanted, so factories are no longer tied to the coal-fields and can be situated wherever conditions are best suited for them.

Africa, with a potential of 145,000 kilowatts of hydro-electric power has the greatest possibilities, followed by Asia with a 140,000 potential.

The most important source of energy of the future is a t o m i c   e n e r g y. The first atomic power plants were erected in Great Britain, the coal deposits there being almost exhausted. (Energy can be extracted from the atom through the fission of very heavy atoms such as uranium in a nuclear reactor; a coolant removes the heat generated in the fission process; this heated gas passes to the boiler in which it converts water to high-pressure steam. The latter drives a turbine which is connected to an electric generator.) The whole apparatus is controlled from a distance, the personnel not going near to the reactor. Great precautions against atomic radiation have to be taken. Waste material has to be buried in the earth or surrounded by concrete and dropped into the deep seas. Atomic-powered submarines can travel long distances without refuelling and so can operate under water for months at a time.

Accidents in nuclear plants, however, have drawn attention to the risks and many governments have been forced to recognize a solid body of opposition to expanding the network. For the first time in its 20-year history, the atomic power industry in the US is fearful for its future. There has never been a disastrous accident in American atomic power plants. Each "nuke" (nuclear power plant) must be designed to withstand the worst earthquakes, floods or other "acts of God". Every piece of equipment meets the stiffest quality controls. Yet the nuclear critics say that there is a disturbing frequeny of small accidents.

A reactor's wastes are so highly radioactive that they pose serious risks to humans. Much of the waste will remain dangerous for centuries. Another byproduct of reactors is plutonium, which can also be used as nuclear fuel. It is the prime ingredient of atomic bombs. Thus the material must be safeguarded so as not to fall into the hands of terrorists or blackmailers.

Nuclear critics say that the economic advantage of "nukes" has turned out to be an illusion. They are more complicated to build than other types of power plants. Atomic power has been considered cheap because of the plant's low operating costs, but "nukes" in the US have been shut down for inspection or repairs on an average of 40% every year. But they play a key part in programmes for national self-sufficiency in energy. Without them, many countries would be at the mercy of foreign oil producers.

A source of energy that will come into its own in the more distant future is s o l a r   e n e r g y, which up to now has remained almost unexploited. Prospects for using solar energy are more favourable in the tropics where the bulk of the world's population lives in the poorest and least-developed countries. It may be used as a cheap, reliable means of cooking food, drying crops, lighting homes, and perhaps of pumping water and powering small factories. U.S. authorities estimate that by the year 2020, 20% of the nations' electricity could be generated by solar energy. There will be solar furnaces, solar engines, solar houses and solar cookers effectively in use in areas with hot climates.

Several countries have tried to harness the p o w e r of the w a v e s and the t i d e s. A French experiment started in 1966 was the first to make use of the tidal ebb by damming the La Rance inlet so the water runs back to the sea through a series of turbines. Since then the U.S., Canada, the Soviet Union, Argentina and Great Britain have put tidal power plants into operation. Geothermal sources such as geysers and volcanic vapours have been successfully harnessed for electric power in such countries as New Zealand, Japan and Iceland.

Incinerating plants which burn garbage or cow dung convert the methane gas derived from it for cooking, lighting and other purposes. China and India lead the way.

Summing up, it would seem that after the dangerous accident in Tschernobyl (U.S.S.R.) in 1986 opposition to atomic power stations is growing world-wide. Oil and natural gas are increasingly costly; the production of coal can be expanded, though mining and burning it cause environment and health problems. The alternative energy sources - sunshine, tides, winds, the earth's heat - are not likely to generate considerable amounts of electricity for decades.

A strong effort to promote energy conservation is surely needed, but the world's need for electricity is steadily growing with the population and industry. The countries of the world have no choice but to use all their possible energy sources.

reserves are dwindling
to meet the demands of the future
to have at one's disposal
concern for the future
finite / infinite
to put the figure at...
gusher
blow-out
oil rig
to serve multiple purposes
to be exhausted
to be extracted from
to convert to / to be converted to
to refuel

a solid body of opposition to...
to meet stiff quality controls
a disturbing frequency of
to pose risks
to safeguard / to be safeguarded
to be considered cheap
low operating costs
to play a key part
self-sufficiency
to be at the mercy of
to come into one's own
to harness / to be harnessed
to lead the way
not likely to
energy conservation
to have no choice but to...

UNEMPLOYMENT

The social revolution and the Welfare State have given many benefits to the workers, one of the most important of these being social security during a time of unemployment. There are still many workers today who can remember the nightmare of unemployment, hunger and misery in the 1930s. At that time there were three million unemployed in Great Britain alone, trying to keep alive on the dole, which was barely enough to support life. Men went without work for years. Their clothes were patched, so they were ashamed of their poverty and became hopeless. They had no money, nothing to do with time, nothing to spend, nothing to wear and they could not get married. They could only stand in the street and watch other men working - crowds of unemployed watching a handful of men working on a road.

With World War II everything changed. After the war there was a time of reconstruction and full employment everywhere. But after the oil crisis in the winter of 1973/74 hard times began again. Suddenly unemployment - not inflation - became Public Enemy No. 1. In December 1974 the number of people out of work in the U.S. was the highest since 1940; the Australian unemployment rate was the worst in 40 years, and the unemployment figures were rising rapidly in Western Europe.

Confidence in the future is sinking rapidly because of new layoffs and plant shutdowns. The car industry (GM, Ford, Chrysler) have laid off over 70,000 autoworkers, who now join the 300,000 already out of work. In Europe the story is the same. The auto-manufacturers in England, Germany and Italy have laid off thousands of workers or put them on a three-day week. Even in Japan, the worldwide economic depression has forced some companies to reduce their work force.

The effects of unemployment on young people are very detrimental. In some countries the numbers of students admitted to universities have to be limited as there is a surplus of out-of-work graduates. In addition to this, it is often not enough for a job-seeker to be trained in one profession or trade, he must have various skills at his finger-tips if he is to find a job easily.

One of the great headaches of today is that jobs are highly specialized, but after the difficult training has been completed, places of work are not easily to be found. After young people complete their training and then become unemployed, they have a feeling of dissatisfaction or frustration, they rebel at the establishment that keeps them out of the work process. This may be a reason why some "drop out" of normal life and join terrorist organizations.

Technical progress in the capitalist system with full automation has proved to be a mixed blessing. Though people have more leisure time, many are replaced at their places of work by computers and other machines. In the nationalized industries the workers are kept on. Instead of becoming redundant (unemployed) they work fewer hours or have to attend courses (with resultant loss of pay). They are not doing productive work and their standard of living is lowered. In totalitarian regimes there is officially no unemployment, but working morale is low as there is no incentive to work hard.

A small London electronics firm recently advertised for an office-boy. Among the 60 applicants were ten out-of-work stockbrokers, three lawyers and several bankers. When the company director told one of the bankers that he looked too grand for the job, the job hunter replied, "I don't mind, I've got a wife and two children to support".

American jobless men with families find it almost impossible to live on the state unemployment compensation (dole) because there are usually no savings to fall back on. Most American families buy their car, TV, refrigerator, etc. on the instalment system (never-never system) and so they have to make large payments every month.

"Without the help from our parents who are on social security", the wife of one unemployed American worker said, "we wouldn't have got through last month".
The jobless rate among blacks in the US is exactly twice the rate for whites. Among teenagers it is high; and even a college degree is no longer an insurance against unemployment.
The trade unions in Europe have now changed their tactics; they no longer push for higher wages, but try to protect the jobs they already have. Here too, a liberal welfare policy softens the blow of unemployment.
Most industrialized societies have created benefit programmes since the Great Depression, which provide an out-of-work employee with a part of his salary for a time. But the rising inflation makes even the highest umemployment benefit seem meager. For working people - blue- and white-collar alike - a depression and time of unemployment is very hard.

to keep alive on the dole
to support life
to become Public Enemy No 1
unemployment rate
unemployment figures
layoffs
plant shutdowns
to lay off workers
to put (workers) on a three-day
   week
to reduce the work force
a surplus of
at one's finger-tips
headache / difficult problem
to drop out
to prove to be
to keep on / to be kept on
redundant / unemployed
resultant

jobless / unemployed / out-of-work
state unemployment compensation
   (dole)
to fall back on (savings)
instalment system (never-never
   system)
to be on social security = Fürsorge-
   rente beziehen
the jobless rate
the trade unions
to push for / demand
a liberal welfare policy
benefit programmes
rising inflation
blue-collar worker = Fabriksarbeiter
white-collar worker = Büroarbeiter

THE TASKS OF A NEUTRAL
AUSTRIA IN EUROPE

Austria became an independent neutral state in 1955. As a neutral country she has various tasks. One of the first of these is to guard her neutrality. In order to do this a country needs an army. Opinions are divided on this point. Some people think that neutrality cannot be protected without a strong army of defence, such as exists in Sweden or Switzerland; this alone can guarantee its neutrality, for whoever is not willing to make a sacrifice for defence has not paid the necessary price for the security, independence and freedom of his country. Others advocate a total disarmament of the smaller states, which should have their neutrality status guaranteed by the great powers. Many people think that it is quite useless for a small country like Austria to have an army as it would not be able to offer resistance against an invading force in the event of war. It is not a question, however, of offering resistance, but a question of the great invading power being forced to start a war. And this is a very difficult decision for any great power to take, for to be an aggressor is to put itself automatically in the wrong. Also, any little war would set off a chain reaction. Herein lies the protection of the independence of the neutral states.

Neutrality also means not to allow one of the great powers of East or West to influence Austria's policy or to monopolize her trade. This requires skilful diplomacy, for Austria must remain on friendly terms with both Eastern and Western European countries.

Austrian firms already do business with both East and West and must exhibit their goods at international fairs all over Europe.

Another task is to promote international co-operation and understanding by becoming a meeting place for congresses and conferences. Vienna is ideally suited for this purpose, situated in the heart of Europe, between West and East. The city is already the seat of many international institutions, including the IAEA (International Atomic Energy Agency) and the UNIDO (United Nations Industrial Development Organization). A large-scale complex has now been completed in Vienna's Danube Park to house both these organisations and to serve as an international conference centre. There is also a permanent conference hall in the Hofburg with a staff of well-trained interpreters. Vienna is a beautiful city and encourages a friendly climate for discussion by its peaceful atmosphere. Delegates from East and West can meet here and work together for peace and progress.

It is also Austria's task to contribute to the unification of Europe by participating in trade associations. Austria already belongs to EFTA (European Free Trade Association), but it is the aim of her political leaders to belong one day to the more powerful association, the Common Market, which includes France, Germany, Great Britain, Italy, the Benelux countries, Denmark and Ireland.

A prominent Austrian politician, speaking at the General Assembly of the Council of Europe at Strassbourg, appealed to the representatives of the European countries to strive for a "European formula" that is not too small or narrow, for "Eastern Europe is also Europe", as he said. He reminded the members that "the inclusion of our country into the economic development of Europe is an indispensable condition for the maintenance of a free and independent Austria." Membership of EFTA has been a benefit for Austria, but our country must also be able to keep pace economically with the other European countries. He continued by emphasizing the contribution that Austria can make towards the easing of East-West relations on account of her geographical position. "We know that a system prevails in the East-European countries that has nothing in common with ours", he said. "But we welcome any development in these countries that gives rise to the hope that they are approaching a conception of a Greater Europe. It is not the Soviet view that extensive co-operation with the Common Market would oppose Austrian State Treaty and neutrality commitments. The Russians know quite well that Austria would not sign anything that does not comply with international commitments and the neutrality status." In conclusion we can say that the Austrian government regards neutrality as a means of preserving Austria's independence and, at the same time, as a stabilising peace-keeping element within the international community.

What Austria can give to the world are works and values which can only grow in an atmosphere of peace.

Austrian policy is also aimed at the improvement of the well-being of the individual and among its foremost tasks are those of a humanitarian nature, especially helping refugees.

opinions are divided
to make a sacrifice
to advocate
to offer resistance
a question of ... ing
to put oneself in the wrong
to take a decision
to set off a chain reaction
herein lies
to monopolize
to remain on friendly terms with
to promote co-operation / under-
    standing

to be suited for a purpose
to contribute to / towards
to participate in
to appeal to
to strive for
indispensable condition
to be of benefit to
to keep pace with
an easing of relations
to prevail
to have in common
to give rise to the hope
commitments
to comply with

M O T O R I Z A T I O N

Motor cars have completely changed our way of life. Let us first look at the advantages that motorization has brought with it. The motor car has improved the lives of the people because it gives them greater freedom, mobility and more choice in where and when to go. City-dwellers can go into the country at week-ends and people living in the country are no longer isolated. Many people drive to und from work because going by car is usually quicker than by public transport. Driving and camping holidays are pleasant because one is free to go or stop wherever one wants and need not worry about booking accomodation in advance.

The motor car industry has created thousands of jobs. It has become a major force in the economy. The complexity of the motor car requires hundreds of different items and so stimulates other industries whose products are needed for cars, such as steel and other metals, glass, natural and synthetic rubber, plastics, textiles and chemicals. The enormous growth of the oil industry is directly connected with the demands of the motor car. The appearance of thousands of repair shops, garages and service stations to maintain, store and supply the cars is also connected with the expansion of the motor car industry. The manufacture, distribution, service and use of motor vehicles are also a major source of revenue to the state, through various special taxes and toll charges.

But cars have not only brought us benefits. Firstly, from an economic point of view, they are a "mixed blessing". The railways, which once held a monopoly of fast transportation, have suffered severely in competition with motor vehicles. The vast expansion in road building with its motorways, bridges and tunnels costs the government enormous sums and has caused a rise in petrol taxes. The high cost of more cars causes many people to buy on the instalment system, thus increasing individual indebtedness.

Apart from these economic aspects, we can see that cars reduce the quality of our environment. The carbon-monoxide in car fumes pollute the air and cause lung-cancer. Life for people living near main roads or motorways is becoming unbearable because of the roar of traffic past their front doors. Towns are made ugly by huge car parks; the country-side is spoilt by road networks. Traffic jams in or near large cities at rush hours get worse and worse. Traffic comes to a standstill and everyone's nerves are frayed.

People become so used to driving everywhere that they grow lazy and almost "lose the use of their legs", which is bad for their health. Driving brings out a man's worst qualities. People who are normally quiet and pleasant may become unrecognizable when they are behind a steering wheel. They are ill-mannered and aggressive and all their hidden frustrations are brought to the surface when driving.

The greatest evil that the car has brought us is the terrible slaughter on the roads. Thousands of people are killed or injured all over the world in traffic accidents each year. A strict world traffic code would have a beneficial effect on the accident rate. For example, the driving test should be made more difficult; drivers should be tested every three years; all vehicles should be put through an annual safety test; drinking and driving laws should be made stricter; there should be maximum and minimum speed limits on all roads and the government should lay down safety specifications for motor car manufacturers.

In the last few years the number of heavy lorries roaring through Austria has increased very fast. The noise and pollution from this traffic has made life in some places unbearable. Steps are being taken to get the lorry traffic off the roads and on the railways. This has already been achieved successfully in Switzerland. Summing up, we can see that the motor car is a mixed blessing and if we are to control the machine in future we must fully realize both the good and the evil that it can do.

to worry / bother about
to create jobs
to be connected with
a source of revenue to the state
toll charges
a "mixed blessing"
to hold a monopoly
to suffer in competition with
in the instalment system
individual indebtedness
the quality of environment

to "lose the use of one's legs" =
    das Gehen verlernen, wörtl.:
    gelähmt werden
to bring out a man's(best, worst)
    qualities
to bring / be brought to the surface
to have a beneficial effect on
    the accident rate
to put (vehicles) through a safety
    test
to lay down safety specifications /
    rules

AIMS IN LIFE

School-leaving is a turning-point in the life of every young person and is, therefore, the time to think about one's aim in life.
Of course, the aim of most people is the "pursuit of happiness", but what comprises happiness? One important factor is the choice of the right profession. People's characters and attitudes towards life vary very much. If someone is ambitious he will want to succeed in his career and rise to the top of his profession. Another may derive satisfaction from having an interesting job and being able to earn enough money to support a family. Yet another may have artistic talents and wish to pursue a career in one of the arts - music, painting, sculpture, acting, etc.
When deciding on what career to take up, one must analyse one's own character and find out one's leanings and limitations. Do you have a creative urge, do you wish to have a responsible position, or will you be content to be an underling all your life? Do you know your own or your parents' financial limitations, and are you willing to make sacrifices in order to pay the costs of a long and difficult training course? If you are a girl, do you want to get married and have children? Will a happy family life give you fulfilment? All these and similar questions must be answered by young people when they are considering their aims in life.

For some people the whole meaning of life is to make more and more money. Why do people want or need money? It is, normally, to have financial security, a life free from care. Apart from the necessities of everyday life, money provides us with luxuries, holidays and entertainment. There is a saying that "the best things of life are free", but this is not quite accurate. Money purchases financial security, without which life can be very hard and squalid. A little money well spent, however, can bring much pleasure. Books are much cheaper today than they used to be. So young people can soon acquire a library of their own. Others who are interested in the theatre can attend performances at very little expense. Those who are keen on music can invest their money in music lessions and in going to concerts. But for some people the acquisition of wealth is an aim of life in itself.

If we consider the lives of some well-known millionaires, we see that they are self-made men. Through untiring industry they have risen to the top of the business world. But many are "workaholics" (work addicts) and are so used to working that they cannot stop. They go on and on acquiring wealth and enlarging their business empires. They have no time for hobbies and have never learnt to relax. Tycoons, like Howard Hughes or J. Paul Getty, become over-suspicious misers and withdraw from the world. Hughes, one of the richest men in the world, spent the last years of his life lying ill in the dark and watching old films, surrounded by parasitic "aides" who did not even call a doctor in time when he was dying. A self-made man often tries to make things easier for his son, who is given everything he wants. So this type of young man may at some time break laws and come into conflict with the police. He expects his father to use his influence and his money to get him out of his scrapes, which the former usually does. (In his play "An Inspector Calls" J.B. Priestley has described this conflict between the self-made Mr. Birling and his son Eric.) Then comes the time when the father retires and expects his son to take over the business. But the son is weak, lazy and imcompetent, business deteriorates and finally he goes bankrupt. From these few examples we can see that money alone cannot bring happiness and it is not right, therefore, to make it the main aim in life.

Many people find fulfilment in the family, in an interesting job, in art, in sport, in helping others, in personal relationships. Friendship can be an important component of happiness. It is good to have loyal friends who will stick to you and not let you down. Good health is also of importance, although many people overcome ill-health and manage to lead full and useful lives. Some want to lead adventurous lives and to travel extensively. Today a lot of young people are disillusioned with the materialistic world they live in and try to "drop out" of it, creating a world of illusion by drugs. Others protest by becoming political fanatics and terrorists. But they are only a small minority.

Summing up, we can say that the nature of a person determines his happiness and, therefore, his aim in life too. Money is not everything - to lead a full and happy life it is necessary to have interesting work, security, a happy family background and loyal friends.

turning-point	... money well spent
pursuit of happiness	at very litte expense
attitude towards life	the acquisition of wealth
to rise to the top of one's profession	in itself
	self-made man
to derive satisfaction from	untiring industry = hard work
to support a family	"workaholics" = work addicts
leanings	tycoon = powerful capitalist
limitations	to make things easier
creative urge	to come into conflict
underling	to get into / out of a scrape
to make sacrifices	to stick to (someone)
free from care	to let (someone) down
	to manage to